# Celtic Jokes

Also by Dilwyn Phillips:

WELSH JOKES

(published in the *It's Wales* series)

First impression: 2003
Copyright © Dilwyn Phillips and Y Lolfa, 2003

Cover design: Sion Jones

ISBN: 0 86243 685 0

*yl Lolfa*

Printed on acid-free and partly recycled paper
and published and bound in Wales by
Y Lolfa Cyf., Talybont, Ceredigion SY24 5AP
*e-mail* ylolfa@ylolfa.com
*website* www.ylolfa.com
*tel* (01970) 832 304
*fax* 832 782

# Contents

# Introduction

The Celts were people who inhabited parts of Western Europe. Their present-day descendants are the Scottish, the Irish, the Manx, the Cornish, and the Welsh.

During the fifth Century the Anglo-Saxons invaded Britain; during this era, the Celts were reputed to have used dye, made from the woad plant, to decorate their bodies. This blue dye, similar to the war paint used by the American Red Indians, was usually painted on the back of the body, with some spaces along the spine for air. During a battle against the Celts, an Anglo-Saxon noticed this characteristic body-painting and similarly painted woad over his own back, hoping to infiltrate the Celts. His ploy was soon discovered by the Celts and upon being captured, he asked how they had foiled his plan. He was told that his disguise had failed because "In Bwitain we have a white wine down the middle of the woad".

All Celts have a sense of humour – the Irishmen laugh and joke about the Kerryman; the Welshmen also about themselves; the Scotsman plays the bagpipes – an instrument allegedly invented by the Irish and given to the Scottish – who still haven't seen through the joke…

The Scots have an (unjustified) reputation for stinginess.

Double glazing is doing great business in Scotland in the hope that children will be unable to hear the ice-cream van when it comes round. The Celts have this ability to joke about themselves... and of course even more so about their neighbours.

I am a true Welshman, but have some poteen in my blood, handed down by ancestors from both parents. I have travelled much of the Celtic lands, met the people, and since my last book, *Welsh Jokes*, have been inundated with these stories about the Irishman, the Scotsman, the Welshman... and of course the Englishman.

Dilwyn Phillips, June 2003

## Kids and Education

Young Tommy missed school on Thursday, so his teacher asked him where he'd been.

"Oh, Miss," replied Tommy, "I've been to my uncle's funeral."

"I'm sorry to hear that," said Miss Jones. "What happened?"

"You see, Miss," said Tommy, "he fell up to his ankles in the slurry pit."

"Well," replied Miss Jones, "surely that wasn't dangerous enough for him to die?"

"He fell in hat-first," replied Tommy.

\* \* \*

The mistress of a big English house called her Irish maid and drew her attention to the dust on top of the piano.

"Mary," she said. "I could write my name in this dust."

Mary responded, "Isn't education a grand thing, ma'am?"

\* \* \*

The teacher asked Tommy, "What do you call a person who keeps on talking when people are no longer interested?" Tommy replied, "A teacher."

\* \* \*

Little Hamish came home from school one day and told his mother he had been given a part in the school play.

"Wonderful," says the mother, "What part is it?"

"I play the part of the Scottish husband!"

The mother scowls and says: "Go back and tell your teacher you want a speaking part."

\* \* \*

Mel was given a side of venison which he gave to his wife to cook for Sunday lunch.

During lunch, he asked the kids if they could guess what they were eating.

Tommy bach guessed beef, which he was told was the wrong answer.

Megan fach guessed pork, again the wrong answer.

Mel decided to give the kids a clue.

"It's something your mum sometimes calls me."

"I know," said Mari fach. "We're eating arsehole."

\* \* \*

Young Dafydd was about eight years old, and went to the corner shop and bought a pretty good-sized box of washing powder. The shopkeeper walked over and, trying to be friendly, asked Dafydd if he had a lot of laundry to do.

"Oh, no laundry," Dafydd said. "I'm going to wash my dog."

"But you shouldn't use this to wash your dog. It's very powerful and if you wash your dog in this, he'll get sick. In fact, it might even kill him."

But Dafydd was not to be stopped. He carried his washing powder to the counter and paid for it, even as the shopkeeper still tried to talk him out of washing his dog. About a week later Dafydd was back in the shop to buy some sweets. The shopkeeper asked Dafydd how his dog was doing.

"Oh, he died," said Dafydd. The shopkeeper, trying not to be an I-told-you-so, said he was sorry the dog died but added, "I tried to tell you not to use that washing powder on your dog."

"Well," replied Dafydd, "I don't think it was the washing powder that killed him."

"Oh? What was it then?"

"I think it was the spin cycle."

\* \* \*

An old country doctor went way out to the hills above Welshpool to deliver a baby.

It was so far out in the countryside that there was no electricity. When he arrived, no one was home except for the heavily pregnant mother, who was about to give birth, and her 5-year-old son Dafydd. The doctor instructed Dafydd to hold a lantern high so he could see, while he helped the mother deliver the baby. Young Dafydd did so with pride. The mother pushed, and after a little while, the doctor lifted the newborn baby by the feet and traditionally spanked him on his bottom to get him to take his first breath. The doctor then asked little Dafydd what he thought of the baby. Dafydd replied: "He shouldn't have crawled in there in the first place. Smack him again."

\* \* \*

The nursery teacher holds up a picture and asks, "What's this?"

"A horsey," answers Megan.

"And this?" the teacher asks.

"A piggy," replies Dafydd.

"And now this one?" asks the teacher, holding up a picture of a male deer with a beautiful rack of antlers. There was no answer, only total silence.

"Come now, children," she coaxes, "I'll give you a little hint. What does your Mummy call your Daddy when he hugs and kisses her a lot?"

"I know! I know!" exclaims Ianto. "It's a horny bastard!"

\* \* \*

A bodhrán player was sick of the band abusing him, and decided to start his own. He walked into a music shop, planning to buy the first instruments he saw.

"I'll take the red saxophone and that accordion," he said. The assistant said, "You play the bodhrán, don't you?"

"That's right. Why?"

"Well, the fire extinguisher I can sell you – but the radiator stays."

\* \* \*

Another bodhrán player was fed up of the other band members talking about time signatures, bars and rhythms and stuff that he didn't understand, and his girlfriend said, "Why don't you get a book about music theory, and study it? Then you'll know what they're talking about and you won't feel left out."

He mulled this over for a while, and decided to go for it. The very next day, he goes to town, musters up some confidence, and goes into the shop, straight up to the assistant, and says, "I'd like a book on music theory, please."

"You're a bodhrán player, aren't you?" said the assistant.

"Yes! How did you know?" said the astounded bodhrán player.

"This is a bloody fish and chip shop, mate. Now piss off."

\* \* \*

Sion bach noticed his mum getting fatter and fatter, until eventually he askes her why she is getting bigger.

"Oh!" exclaims his mum. "You see, Sion, I've got a little baby in my tummy."

Sion was really bewildered by this and asked his mummy how she got it.

"You see, Sion, your father gave it to me"

Sion bach was amazed, and couldn't wait for his father to get home from work.

"Daddy," enquired Sion, "did you really give mummy a baby?"

"Why, yes," replied his father.

"Do you know what, daddy? She's gone and bloody eaten it."

\* \* \*

"Mother," asks Sean looking through the wedding album, "who's the big chunky chap with the long hair at your wedding?"

"Oh, to be sure," said his mother, "it's your dad."

"Is it?" retorts Sean. "Then who's the bald fat fella living with you now, then?"

* * *

A first-year student from the Isle of Skye, called Donald MacDonald, was studying at an English university. He was living in the hall of residence and after he'd been there a month, his mother came to visit, carrying reinforcements of scones and oatmeal.

"And how do you find the English students, Donald?" she asked.

"Mother," he replied. "They're such terribly noisy people. The one on that side keeps banging his head against the wall, and won't stop. The one on the other side screams and screams and screams, away into the night."

"Oh, Donald! How do you manage to put up with these awful noisy English neighbours?"

"Mother, I do nothing. I just ignore them. I just stay here quietly, playing my bagpipes."

* * *

Tomos opened the big family bible. He was fascinated as he fingered through the old pages. Suddenly, something fell out of the bible. He picked up the object and looked at it. What he saw was an old leaf that had been pressed in between the pages.

"Mammy, look what I found," Tomos shouted.

"What have you got there, cariad?" With astonishment in his voice, he answered, "I think it's Adam's underwear!"

* * *

A few days after Christmas, Dai's mother was working in the kitchen listening to Dai playing with his new electric train set in the living room. She heard the train stop, and her son yelled, "All you bastards who want to get off, get out now, because this is the last stop! All of you bastards that are getting on, shift your arses, 'cause we're leaving".

Dai's Mam went in and said, "We don't use that kind of language in this house. Now I want you to go into your room for two hours. When you come out, you can play with your train, but I don't want to hear any bad language."

Two hours later, Dai came out of his room and continued playing with his train. Soon, the train stopped and his mother heard her son say, "All passengers who are disembarking from the train, please remember to take all your belongings with you. We thank you for travelling with us today and hope your ride was a pleasant one. We hope you will ride with us again soon. For those of you who are just boarding the train, we ask that you stow all of your hand luggage under the seat. Remember, there is no smoking except in the club car. We hope you have a pleasant and relaxing journey with us today. For those of you who are pissed off with the two hour delay, please see the bitch in the kitchen."

\* \* \*

A wee lad, just getting home from school runs up to his dad.

"Daddy, Daddy! I'm the only one in my class that can count to ten. Why do you reckon so?"

"Why, I reckon its because you're from Glasgow, Angus." his dad responds.

The next day the wee lad gets home from school.

"Daddy, Daddy! I'm the only one in my class that knows all the letters in the alphabet. Why do you reckon so?"

"I reckon it's because you're from Glasgow Angus." His dad tells him again.

The next day the wee lad busts through the door.

"Daddy. Daddy! I'm the only one in school who has a large penis, is that because I'm from Glasgow?" His dad looks at him and says, "No. Angus. I reckon its because you're twenty two."

\* \* \*

Mrs ap Rhewgell was having a hard time with her son, Seisyllt. Whenever her friends came to visit, Seisyllt would rush at them, grab their legs, and sink his teeth into them, refusing to let go. This disturbed behaviour caused considerable distress – not to mention embarrassment – to Mrs ap Rhewgell, and she decided to take Seisyllt to see a child psychologist.

Upon entering the child psychologist's room, Seisyllt immediately rushed up to him, wrapped his arms around his legs and sank his teeth into his flesh. The psychologist calmly bent down and whispered a few words into Seisyllt's ear, upon which Seisyllt released the psychologist's leg and ran to hide behind his mother.

"Gosh!" said his mother. "What an amazing cure! How on earth did you manage that?"

"I told him that if he didn't let my legs go, I'd kick the shit out of him."

\* \* \*

Reaching the end of a job interview, the personnel officer asked a young engineer from Furnace, newly qualified and fresh out of Treforest, "What starting salary are you looking for?"

The young engineer replied, "In the region of £40,000 a year, depending on the benefits package."

The interviewer said, "Well, what would you say to a benefit package of 6 weeks' paid holiday leave, full medical and dental treatment, company matching retirement fund to 75% of salary, and a company car leased every 2 years – say, a Porsche 944?"

The engineer sat up straight and said, "Wow! Are you kidding?"

The interviewer replied, "Yes, but you started it."

\* \* \*

How do you know when there's a bodhrán player at the door? The knocking is very loud and speeds up, and he never knows when to come in.

\* \* \*

Miss Jones took her class to the swimming pool for their weekly lessons. After all the kids were enjoying themselves, she approached Gomer bach and said, "Gomer, you mustn't pee pee in the swimming pool.

"But Miss," replies Gomer, "everyone else does it."

"I know, Gomer," replies Miss Jones, "but not from the diving board."

\* \* \*

One day, Miss Jones told her class that they were not to use childish words, and insisted that no baby talk was allowed, only grown-up words. She asked Dafydd bach what he did on the weekend.

"Please Miss," he answered, "I went to visit Nana."

"No," said Miss Jones, "you went to visit your grandmother. You must learn to use grown-up words." She asked Bethan what she did.

"Please Miss," answered Bethan, "I went for a ride on the choo choo."

"No, Bethan," corrected Miss Jones, "you went for a ride on the train. You must learn to use grown up words. And what did you do, Gareth?" she asked.

"Please Miss, I read a book," replied Gareth.

"Good," said Miss Jones, "What did you read, Gareth bach?"

Gareth thought for a moment, and said, "Winnie the Shit."

\* \* \*

The Biology teacher asked her class what they knew about the birds and the bees. With that, Barry started crying.

"What's wrong, Barry?" said Miss Williams.

"Miss," he replied, "when I was eight, I was told that there was no Father Christmas. When I was nine, I was told that there was no Easter bunny. When I was ten, I was told that there was no tooth fairy, and I suppose now your going to tell me that grown ups don't really have sex. There's nothing left to live for now."

\* \* \*

Young Hamish and his friend Angus went to the cinema and, before the film, went to the toilets to relieve themselves. Hamish weed, then washed his hands, but much to his surprise he saw that Angus did not wash his.

"Hey," said Hamish, "smart boys wash their hands after they pee."

Holding his head back proudly, young Angus corrected, "Smart boys learn not to pee on their hands."

\* \* \*

Angus asked his father, "Dad, where did I get my intelligence from?"

His father replied, "You must have got it from your mother. I still have mine."

# Women

Liam was found dead in his back yard, and as the weather was a bit on the warm side, the wake was held down to only two days, so his mortal remains wouldn't take a bad turn. At last his friends laid him in the box, nailed it shut and started down the hill into the churchyard. As it was a long, sloping path and the mourners were appropriately tipsy, one fellow lurched into the gatepost as they entered the graveyard. Suddenly a loud knocking came from inside the box. Liam was alive! They opened the box up, and he sat up wide-eyed, and they all said, "Sure, it's a miracle of God!" All rejoiced, and they went back and had a few more drinks, but later that day, poor Liam died. Really died. Stone cold dead. They bundled him back into his box, and as they huffed and puffed down the hill the next morning, the priest said, "Careful now, boys; mind ye don't bump the gatepost again."

\* \* \*

"Well, Mrs Jones, so you want a divorce?" the solicitor questioned his client. "Tell me about it. Do you have a grudge?"

"Oh, no," replied Mrs. Jones. "Sure now, we only have a carport."

The solicitor tried again. "Well, does the man beat you up?"

"No, no," said Mrs Jones, looking puzzled. "I'm always first out of bed."

Still hopeful, the solicitor tried once again: "Well, does he go in for unnatural connubial practices?" "Well, now you say that, he plays the flute, but I don't think he knows anything about the connubial."

Now desperate, the solicitor pushed on. "What I'm trying to find out are what grounds you have." "Bless you, sir. We live in a flat – not even a window box, let alone grounds.

"Mrs. Jones," the solicitor said in considerable exasperation, "you need a reason that the court can consider. What is the reason for you seeking this divorce?"

"Ah, well now," said the lady, "you see, it's because the man can't hold an intelligent conversation."

\* \* \*

Four ladies from Carmarthen board a train for a long journey to a W.I. conference. Shortly into the trip, one of the ladies says, "Well, we've all worked together for many years, but we don't really know one another. I suggest we tell each other one of our sins."

They look nervously at each other, but nod agreement. The first lady says, "Since I suggested it, I'll go first. With me, it's the secret drinking. Once a year I go out of town to a pub and drink myself blind for a few days and end up staying the night. Get it out of my system."

They all look each other again nervously, but the next lady slowly starts, "With me, it's gambling. Periodically, I nick the money out of the W.I. collection box and go to the races. Spend it all! I get it out of my system."

The third, who is really nervous, now reluctantly says, "This is very difficult. My sin is worse. I let my hair down and go into the red light district, go on the game, and spend a week in the saddle. I REEEEAAALLY get it out of my system."

They all look at the fourth lady, waiting. She doesn't say anything. Then one of the four speaks up, "Come now, we've all told our innermost faults. It's your turn."

She looks at the others and starts hesitantly, "Well… I'm an inveterate gossip, and I can't wait to get off this bloody train!"

\* \* \*

Three times Myfanwy took Ianto to the manse, hoping to be made man and wife, but each time the preacher refused because of the groom-to-be's intoxicated state.

"Why do you persist in bringing him to me in such a state?" asked the preacher.

"Please, Mr Evans," explained Myfanwy, "He won't come when he's sober."

\* \* \*

Rhiannon, a blonde from Cowbridge, pulls into her drive and walks into the house. She smells smoke as she opens the door and discovers that her house is on fire. She grabs the phone, dials 999, and asks for the fire brigade to report the fire. The operator answers and Rhiannon screams frantically, "Help, my house is on fire!"

The operator tries to calm Rhianon and asks her what her address is.

"123 William Street. Please hurry!" The operator asks, "How do we get there?"

She replies, "Duh! In a big red fire engine!"

\* \* \*

A speed cop pulls up alongside a speeding car on the A487. Glancing at the car, he is astounded to see that the blonde behind the wheel is knitting! Realizing that she was oblivious to his flashing lights and siren, the speedcop cranks down his window and yelled, "Pull over!"

"No," the blonde yelled back, "it's a scarf!"

\* \* \*

John the Gas is at home watching Manchester playing on the telly, when his partner Nia interrupts:

"Could you fix the fridge door? It won't close properly." John responds, "Fix the fridge door? Have I got Zanussi written on my forehead? I don't think so!"

"Fine!" says Nia, "Then could you at least fix the steps to the front door? They're about to break".

"Have I got Ronseal written on my forehead? I don't think so! I've had enough of this, I'm going to the Llew Gwyn to see the match!" So he goes to the pub and drinks for a couple of hours. When he arrives home, he notices that the steps are fixed. He goes to the fridge to get a beer and notices that the fridge door is also fixed.

"Cariad, how'd this all get fixed?"

"Well," she says, "when you left, I sat outside and cried. Just then, a nice and very handsome young man asked me what was wrong, so I told him. He offered to do all the repairs, and all I had to do was bake him a cake, or have sex with him."

"So, what kind of cake did you bake him?" he asked.
She replied: "Hello! Have I got Mr Kipling written on my forehead? I don't think so!"

* * *

Two women go out one weekend without their husbands. As they came back, right before dawn, both of them drunk, they felt the urge to pee. They noticed the only place to stop was a cemetery. Though it was a little scary, they decided to go there anyway. The first one had nothing to clean herself with, so she took off her panties and used them to clean herself and discarded them. The second waman, also unable to find anything, thought "I'm not getting rid of my panties," so she used the ribbon of a flower wreath to clean herself.

The morning after, the two husbands were talking to each other on the phone, and one says to the other: "We have to be on the look-out; it seems that these two were up to no good last night. My wife came home without her panties." The other one responded: "You're lucky, mine came home with a card stuck to her ass that read, 'We will never forget you'".

Megan is trying her written driving test consisting of yes/no type questions. She takes her seat in the examination hall, stares at the question paper for five minutes and then, in a fit of inspiration, takes her purse out, removes a coin and starts tossing the coin, marking the answer sheet: 'yes' for heads, and 'no' for tails.

Within half an hour she is all done, whereas the rest of the class is still sweating it out. During the last few minutes she is seen desperately throwing the coin, muttering and sweating. The moderator, alarmed, approaches, her and asks what is going on. "I finished the exam in half an hour, but I'm rechecking my answers."

* * *

Blodwen goes to the lonely hearts column of the *South Wales Mail* and enquires about placing an advert in the lonely hearts column.

"Certainly," said the assistant, "that's £1 per insertion."

"Is that all?" replied Blodwen. "Forget the advert. I'll have £20's worth."

* * *

A blonde girl from Plasmarl decided to have a wild evening and rented a video from the local video shop.

She opened a bottle of champagne, lit some candles, and wore some erotic underwear to watch her special film. Much to her disappointment, all she managed to see was static. The following day, she returned to the shop to complain.

"I rented a film from you last night," she said, "and all I could see was white static."

"Sorry about that," said the assistant. "Which film was it?"

"Head Cleaner."

* * *

Dai and Blodwen are celebrating their fiftieth wedding anniversary. Dai turned to Blodwen and said, "Blod bach, I was wondering – have you ever cheated on me?" Blodwen replies, "Dai, why would you be asking such a question after fifty years of happy marriage? You don't want to ask that question."

"Yes, Blod fach, I really want to know. Please."

"Well, all right. Yes, three times."

"Three times? Well, when?" he asked.

"Well, Dai, remember when you were 35 years old and you really wanted to buy a shop and no bank would give you a loan? Remember, then one day Mr Ianto Evans, the bank manager himself came over the house and signed the loan papers, no questions asked?"

"Oh, Blod fach, you did that for me! I respect you even more than ever, to do such a thing for me. So, when was number two?"

"Well, Dai, remember when you had that last heart attack and you were needing that very tricky operation, and no surgeon would touch you? Then remember how Dr Williams, the heart specialist, came all the way up here, to do the surgery himself, and then you were in good shape again?"

"I can't believe it! Blod fach, you should do such a thing for me, to save my life. I couldn't have a more wonderful wife. To do such a thing, you must really love me darling. I couldn't be more moved. So, all right then, when was number three?"

"Well, Dai, remember a few years ago, when you really wanted to join the golf club and you were 23 votes short?"

\* \* \*

Meinir announces to her friend that she is getting married for the fourth time. "How wonderful! But I hope you don't mind me asking what happened to your first husband?"

"He ate poisonous mushrooms and died."

"Oh, how tragic! What about your second husband?"

"He too ate poisonous mushrooms and died."

"Oh, how terrible! I'm almost afraid to ask you about your third husband."

"He died of a broken neck."

"A broken neck?"

"He wouldn't eat the mushrooms."

* * *

Myfanwy told Marged, "I've got to get some contraceptive pills immediately. I can't afford to get pregnant."

"But," Marged said, "I thought Ianto had had a vasectomy."

"He has," replied Myfanwy, "and that's why I can't afford to get pregnant."

* * *

Coleen walks into the kitchen to find Mickey wandering about with a fly swatter in his hand.

"What are you doing, Mickey?" she asked.

"I'll be after these flies, my dearie," he replied.

"Have you caught any yet?" she retorted.

"Aye, two males and three females," replied Mickey.

"And how can you tell their sex?" asked Coleen.

"There were two on a beer can, and three on the telephone, dear."

# Men

There is an old couple in the Rhondda, Marged and Iwan. Marged joins Iwan in the living room and says, "Iwan, oh, I am so proud of you, so proud. Last month, I told you that you were spending too much time at the pub, and too much time away from me. Since then, you haven't gone to the pub once, and stayed home. I want to do something special for you; I want to make you a special dinner, special indeed." Iwan replied, "Oh, Marged, you don't have to do that, don't trouble yourself."

"No, it's no trouble," Marged insisted, "In fact, when we were on holiday in Brittany last year, you really enjoyed that escargot. You go to the Spar and get them snails, and I'll cook them in garlic for you, the way you liked them." Iwan got excited, "Oh, that would be fantastic! OK, I'll go straight away."

So Iwan goes to the Spar to get the snails, but has to pass the Angel on the way. As he passes, everyone in the pub starts yelling, "Hey, Iwan boy! Where've you been, butty? Come on in, and let me buy you a pint!"

"No, no, no, no. I've got to get to the Spar. No, I've got to go."

They keep it up, "C'mon, Iwan, just one. Let me buy you one!"

Iwan answers, "No, no, no, I've got to go," and makes it to the shop and gets the snails. On his way back he has to pass the Angel once again, and they start again, "Hey, Iwan! Come on in and let me buy you a pint!" Iwan answers, "No, no, no, no. I've got to get home. No, I've got to go." They beg, "C'mon butty, just one." Iwan responds, "No, I've got to go. I've got to... well, just one."

By the time Iwan checks the time, it's 11.00 p.m.

"Oh, no! I've got to go!" he exclaims. Iwan starts running home, gets to the gate, flings it open, and then trips. The snails go flying everywhere. Marged hears the noise and comes out and yells, "Iwan! It's after 11 o'clock! What took you so long? Where have you been?!?"

Iwan looks up at Marged, looks down and sees the snails spread out everywhere, gets up, waves and exclaims, "Come on, boys, keep it going! We're almost there!"

* * *

What do bodhrán players use for birth control?
Their personalities.

* * *

What's the best thing to play a bodhrán with?
A razor blade.

* * *

Fellow walks into a pub in Belfast with a plastic bag under his arms.

The bartender asks, "What's that?"

"Six pounds of semtex," he answers.

"Thanks be to Jaysus; I thought it was a bodhrán!"

* * *

Then there was the bodhrán player who remembered that he had left his bodhrán in his unlocked car. Rushing back, he opened his car door to find two more bodhráns in the back seat.

* * *

What do you call an aggressive groupie who hangs around, annoying session musicians?
A bodhrán player.

* * *

What's the difference between a bodhrán and a trampoline?
You take off your shoes when you jump on a trampoline.

* * *

Bodhrán care is simple... Rub gently with lighter fluid and ignite.

* * *

Then of course there was the fiddle player who, while visiting the local pub, was asked for a dollar to help pay for the funeral of a local bodhrán player. "Here's two dollars," he says, "bury another."

* * *

Is a bodhrán player a musician?
Is a barnacle a ship?

* * *

What's the difference between a bodhrán player and a foot massage?
A foot massage bucks up the feet, whereas…

* * *

Q. Why do bagpipers walk when they play?
A. To get away from the sound.

* * *

What do you get when you play Irish music backwards?
Irish music.

* * *

Angus was asked why there were drones on the bagpipe when they make such a distressing sound. He answered, "Without the drones, I might as well be playing the piano."

* * *

Myfanwy followed her Ianto to the public house. "How can you come here," she said, taking a sip of his pint of bitter, "and drink that awful stuff?"

"Now!" he cried. "Myfanwy, and you are the one who always said I was out enjoying myself."

* * *

Did you hear about the two Cardiffians who were stopped by the police for being drunk and disorderly? It turned out that the first had been drinking battery acid and the second had been swallowing fireworks.

One was charged and the other was let off.

* * *

Angus went into a shop to buy a pocketknife.

"We've got the very thing for you," said the shopkeeper, "six blades and a corkscrew."

"Tell me," said Jock, "you haven't one with six corkscrews and a blade, have you?"

* * *

It was cold on the upper deck and the captain was concerned for the comfort of his passengers.

He called down: "Is there a mackintosh down there big enough to keep two young lassies warm?"

"No, skipper," came the reply, "but there's a McPherson willing to try."

* * *

"You know, bonny sweetheart, since I met you, I can't eat, I can't sleep, can't drink my whisky…"

"Why not, Hamish? "

"I'm broke."

* * *

An Englishman decides to have some fun at the locals' expense. Seeing a rustic Cornish fellow at work in a garden he calls out, "I say my man! I don't suppose you've seen a cart load of monkeys around here?"

The gardener replied, "Why? Falled off 'ave 'e?"

* * *

A Welsh miner fell down a coalmine shaft. His fellow miners called down the shaft to him, "Anythin' broken, Dai?"

"No," he replied. "There's nothin' down here but a few rocks."

* * *

Farmer Ifans remarks to his wife, "When I passed the barn, Twm had hanged 'imself from a beam."

"Did you cut him down?" said the wife.

"No, he wasn't dead yet," said the farmer.

* * *

It was hay time and the top-heavy cart coming from the field had overturned in the lane. Its young driver, Dai Bach, looked at the fallen load in dismay.

"Come in for a dish of tea," said a motherly soul to the boy as he stood there. "We'll give you a hand putting it right afterwards. You'll feel more like loading again after a drink and a sit down."

"Dad won't like it," said Dai Bach doubtfully.

"He won't know anything about it," said the woman comfortingly and led the boy, still reluctant, into the house to join her family. Half an hour later, all emerged to view the situation, the lad thanking the lady but repeating that his father wouldn't like it at all.

"Rubbish," she said, "I'll deal with your father. Where's 'e to?"

"Under the hay," said Dai Bach.

* * *

"I always go to funerals," said an old dear from Fishguard when asked if she was going to a neighbour's funeral. "It's like this, see; if you don't go to the other folks' funerals, they won't come to yours."

* * *

A Scottish couple were sitting by the kitchen fire one dark evening when the wife said to her husband: "Open the door an' see if it's rainin' outside".

The husband replied: "Why don't you call the dog in an' see if he's wet?"

* * *

Liam and an American were sitting in the bar at Shannon Airport.

"I've come to meet my brother," said Liam. "He's due to fly in from America in an hour's time. It's his first trip home in forty years".

"Will you be able to recognize him?" asked the American.

"I'm sure I won't," said Liam, "after all, he's been away for a long time."

"I wonder if he'll recognize you?" said the American.

"Of course he will," said Liam. "Sure, I haven't been away at all."

* * *

An Englishman went to a vending machine and arrived there just before a Scotsman came to quench his thirst. He opened his wallet and took out a 50p coin, studied the machine a little, pushed a Diet Coke selection, and out came a Diet Coke, which he placed on a counter by the machine. Then he pulled out another 50p coin and inserted it in the machine. Studying the machine carefully, he pushed the button for Coke Classic and out came a Coke Classic. He immediately put another 50p coin in the machine, studied it for a moment and pushed the Fanta button. Out came a Fanta. As he was reaching for more change, the Scotsman who had been waiting patiently for several minutes now spoke up.

"Excuse me, sir. But are you done yet?" The Englishman looked at him and indignantly replied: "Can't you see? I'm still winning!"

* * *

While hunting in the Highlands, a solicitor from Glasgow brought down a grouse, which landed in a farmer's field. As the lawyer climbed over the wall to retrieve the bird, the elderly owner appeared, and asked what he was doing. The litigator replied, "I shot that grouse you see lying there, and now I'm about to pick it up." The old man answered, "This is my land you're crossing into, and I'm telling you, you're not coming over." The indignant attorney said, "I'll have you know that I'm one of the best solicitors in all of Scotland, and if you don't let me retrieve my grouse, I'll take ye to court for everything you own!" The old farmer looked him over and said, "Well now, being as how you're not from around here, you don't know how we settle things like this. Ye see now, here we use the three-kick method."

"And what would that be?" asked the lawyer. The farmer said, "First I kick you three times, and then you do the same to me, and back and forth like that 'till one or the other gives up." The attorney thought this over, and quickly decided he could easily take the old codger, and agreed to the local custom. The old farmer walked slowly over to the lawyer. His first kick planted the toe of his heavy boot in the solicitor's groin dropping him to his knees. The second blow nearly wiped the lawyer's nose off his face. He was flat on the ground when the farmer's third kick to the kidney almost finished him. The lawyer dug deep for his every bit of will, dragged himself standing, and said, "Okay, you old bugger, now it's my turn." The old farmer just smiled and said, "No, I believe I'll give up now. You can have the grouse."

\* \* \*

Mary McTavert is home as usual, making dinner, when big Rob arrives at her door.

"Mary, may I come in?" he asks. "I've something to tell ye."

"Of course you can come in, you're always welcome, Rob. But

where's my Andy?"

"That's what I'm here to tell you, Mary. There was an accident down at the distillery."

"Oh, God no!" cries Mary. "Please don't tell me."

"But I must, Mary. Your Andy is dead and gone. I'm sorry." Mary reached a hand out to her side, found the arm of the rocking chair by the fireplace, pulled the chair to her and collapsed into it. She wept for many minutes. Finally she looked up at Rob.

"How did it happen, Rob?"

"It was terrible, Mary. He fell into a vat of whisky and drowned."

"Oh my dear Jesus! But you must tell me true, Rob. Did he at least go quickly?"

"Well, no Mary, no."

"No?"

"Fact is, he got out three times for a piss."

* * *

Hamish is working at a sewerage. It's a warm day, so he takes off his jacket and drapes it over a handrail – where it slips off into a vast tank of shite! He's just about to dive in when Angus shouts, "It's nae guid tae do that; the jacket's ruined."

Hamish replies, "Aye, ah ken, but ma sandwiches are in the pocket."

* * *

Evan turned around to Ianto and complained to him that he was rather concerned – he'd received a letter from a man who said if he didn't stop seeing his wife, he'd break his legs.

"Well, Evan," replied Ianto, "are you going to stop seeing her?"

"It's not as easy as that," replied Evan, "he didn't sign the letter."

* * *

Andy wants a job as a signalman on the railways. He is told to meet the inspector at the signal box. The inspector puts this question to him: "What would you do if you realised that two trains were heading for each other on the same track?"

"I would switch the points for one of the trains," Andy says.

"What if the lever broke?" asked the inspector.

"Then I'd dash down out of the signal box," said Andy, "and I'd use the manual lever over there."

"What if that had been struck by lightning?"

"Then," Andy continues, "I'd run back into the signal box and phone the next signal box."

"What if the phone was engaged?"

"Well, in that case," persevered Andy, "I'd rush down out of the box and use the public emergency phone at the level crossing up there."

"What if that was vandalised?"

"Oh well, then I'd run into the village and get my uncle Silas."

This puzzles the inspector, so he asks, "Why would you do that?"

Came the answer, "Because he's never seen a train crash."

* * *

Dai spends a week at his new office with the manager he is replacing. On the last day, the departing manager tells Dai, "I have left three numbered envelopes in the desk drawer. Open an envelope if you encounter any problem or a crisis you can't solve."

Three months down the line there is a major drama, everything goes wrong – the usual stuff – and Dai feels very threatened by it all. He remembers the parting words of his predecessor and opens the first envelope. The message inside says, "Blame your predecessor!" Dai does this and gets off the hook.

About six months later, the company is experiencing a dip in sales, combined with serious product problems. Dai quickly opens the second envelope. The message reads, "Reorganize!" This he does, and the company quickly rebounds.

Three months later, at his next crisis, Dai opens the third envelope. The message inside says 'Prepare three envelopes'.

\* \* \*

Brian drives to a petrol station outside Carmarthen and fills his tank with petrol. While doing this the petrol attendant spots three monkeys sitting in the back of the van. He asks Brian, "What are you doing with the monkeys in the back of your van?" Brian says, "I found them, but I haven't a clue what to do with them." The attendant then suggests, "You should take them to the zoo."

"Yeah, that's a good idea," says Brian, jumps in the van, and drives away. The next day Brian is back at the same petrol station. The attendant sees the monkeys are still in the back of the van and comments, "Hey, they're still here! I thought you were going to take them to the zoo."

"Oh, I did," says Brian, "and we had a fantastic time! Today I'm taking them to the pictures."

\* \* \*

Dafydd: That fellow over in the corner of the pub – I wonder where he is from?
Grandad Twm: I'll go ask him. Hello stranger, where are you from?
Stranger: I'm not from here.
Grandad Twm: First time here then, eh?
Stranger: Never have I been here before.
Grandad Twm: Where do you go to church?
Stranger: Not to the one across the street from the house, that's for sure.
Grandad Twm: Do you like Welsh choirs?
Stranger: I don't like opera.
Grandad Twm: Do you drink Welsh beer?
Stranger: I'm not drinking whisky.

Grandad Twm: Are you a member of the visiting rugby team?
Stranger: Yes, I'm not.
Dafydd: Did you find out where he is from?
Grandad Twm: He's OK, he's a Welshman.

* * *

Hamish buys his mother-in-law a plot in the local cemetery one Christmas. The following year he doesn't buy her anything. When she saw him next, she mentioned the fact that he hadn't bought her anything to which he replied, "You didn't use the present that I bought you last year!"

# Country Folk

In the Northern Highlands, an impatient farmer knocked at the door of neighbouring farmhouse. The daughter of the house answered.

"Is your father in?" asked the neighbour.

"No," said the daughter. "He's at the Inverness farmers' market. If it's the services of the red Ayrshire bull you want, the cost is £50.00."

"No, it's not that," said the neighbour.

"Well," said the daughter, "If it's the Galloway belted bull you want, it's £40."

"No, it's not that," said the neighbour.

"How about the small Highland bull?" said the daughter. "The service of that bull is only £30."

The neighbour rudely interrupted the daughter. "That's not what I've come about. Your brother Angus has made my daughter Barbera pregnant. My wife and I want to know what your father proposes to do about it."

"Oh, well," said the daughter. "You'll have to see my father yourself. I don't know what he charges for Angus."

\* \* \*

Landlord of the White Lion: The room is £15 a night, or £5 if you make your own bed.

Aled: I'll make my own bed.

Landlord of the White Lion: Good. I'll get you some nails and wood.

\* \* \*

Dai, a farmer from Penuwch phones Cardiff Airport and asks, "Is that BA?"

"Yes, it is," came the reply.

"Could you please tell me how long does it take to fly from Cardiff to London?" he asks.

"Just a minute," came the reply.

"Thank you very much," said Dai and put the phone down.

\* \* \*

A burglar breaks into a house in the Rhondda. He sees a CD player that he wants, so he takes it. Then he hears a voice: "Jesus is watching you". He looks around with his flashlight, wondering, "what the hell was that?" He spots some cash on a table and takes it. Once again he hears a voice: "Jesus is watching you". He hides in a corner trying to find where the voice came from. He spots a birdcage with a parrot in it. He goes over and asks,

"Was that your voice?"

"Yes," it replies. The burglar asks, "What's your name?"

"Moses," replies the parrot. The burglar says, "What kind of person names his bird 'Moses'?"

"The same kind of person that names his Rottweiler 'Jesus'."

\* \* \*

Ianto from Bwlch-y-groes has just bought a new MG sports car and is out for a drive when he accidentally cuts off a farmer on a tractor at Synod Inn. The farmer signals for him to pull over. Ianto does so, and the farmer gets out of his tractor and pulls a piece of chalk from his pocket. He drew a circle on the side of the road and gruffly commands Ianto, "Stand in that circle and don't move!" He then goes to Ianto's car and cuts up the leather seats.

When he turns around, Ianto has a slight grin on his face.

"Oh, you think that's funny? Watch this!" The farmer gets a spanner out of his tractor and breaks every window in Ianto's MG.

When he turns around, Ianto has a smile on his face. The farmer's getting really mad, and gets his knife back out and slices all the tyres. Now Ianto's laughing. The farmer is really starting to lose it. He goes back to his tractor and gets a can of paraffin, pours it on the MG and sets it on fire. He turns around and Ianto is laughing so hard, he is almost falling over.

"What's so funny?" the farmer asks Ianto. He replies, "Every time you weren't looking, I stepped outside the circle!"

\* \* \*

One day Mari fach brings her boyfriend home and tells her father she wants to marry him. After talking to him for a while, he tells Mari she can't do it because he's her half-brother. The same thing happens again four more times with four other blokes! Mari starts to get pissed off. She goes to her mother and says, "Mam. What have you been doing all your life? Daddy's been going around every woman in the valley, and now I can't marry any of the five blokes I like because it turns out they're my half-brothers!" Her mother replies, "Don't worry, cariad, you can marry any one of them you want. He isn't really your dad."

\* \* \*

Dai, slightly inebriated after a good night out, is standing out on the street corner when the local bobby passes and says, "Hi, Dai. What do you think you're doing so early in the morning?" Dai says, "I heard the world goes around every 24 hours, and I'm waiting for my house. Won't be long now – there goes my neighbour."

\* \* \*

An Englishman was going for a job interview in Tregaron and on the way out he asked a local farmer for directions: "Excuse me, dude, could you possibly tell me the quickest way to Tregaron?"

The farmer said: "You driving or walking, boyo?"

The Englishman replied: "Driving." The farmer nodded, saying: "Yes, definitely the quickest way."

* * *

A police officer stops Berwyn for speeding and asks him very nicely if he could see his license. Berwyn replies in a huff, "I wish you guys would get your act together. Just yesterday you take away my license and then today you expect me to show it to you!"

* * *

Young Twm from Lampeter goes out for a walk. He comes to a river and sees Dai on the opposite bank. "Hey," he shouts, "how do I get to the other side?" Dai looks up the river then down the river then shouts back, "You are on the other side."

* * *

Dai was playing Trivial Pursuit in the Lion, Treorchy one night. It was his turn. He rolled the dice and it landed on Science and Nature. The question was, 'If you are in a vacuum and someone calls your name, can you hear it?' He thought for a time and then asked, "Is it on or off?"

* * *

Ianto the vet had had a really rough day at his office. When he finally got home from tending to all the sick animals, his wife was waiting with a long cool drink and a romantic candle-lit dinner, after which they had a few more drinks and went happily to bed. At about 1.00 in the morning, the phone rang. "Is that you, Ianto?" asked an elderly woman's voice.

"Yes, it is," replied Ianto, out of breath. "Is this an emergency?"

"Well, sort of," said the elderly voice, "there are cats on the roof outside making a terrible noise mating and I can't get to sleep. What can I do about it?" There was a sharp intake of breath from Ianto, who then patiently replied, "Open the window and yell that they are wanted on the phone."

"Really?" said the woman, "Will that stop them?"

"Should do," said Ianto, "It just stopped me!"

* * *

Twm had a rather nasty accident and died in a fire, which burnt
his body pretty badly. The police found his two friends Gomer
and Watcyn to try to identify the body in the town morgue.
Gomer went in, looked at the body but it was so badly burnt that
he couldn't identify it. He asked the mortician to roll the body
over for a further inspection. Gomer then said, "No, that's not our
Twm."

Watcyn thenwent in. He couldn't identify Twm either, and
likewise asked the mortician to turn the body over, then said,
"That's not Twm."

The mortician then asked them both how they were so sure that
the body was not Twm's.

"Well," replied Gomer, "everybody in Carmarthen knew Twm
had two arseholes."

"What?!" said the mortician in astonishment.

"Yes," replied Watcyn , "wherever the three of us went, people
would say, 'Here comes Twmwith them two arseholes'!"

* * *

Ithel was showing his horses at the Royal Welsh, during the Prince
of Wales's visit, and as he was proudly showing his best cob, it
broke wind.

"I'm sorry about that, your highness," said Ithel in
embarrassment.

"That's all right," said the Prince, "If you hadn't apologised, I
would have assumed it was the horse that had farted."

* * *

Megan was walking home to Llanbrynmair one evening when she
met Morgan walking in the same direction. Megan said to
Morgan, "You know, Morgan, I'm almost afraid of walking home
with you, in case you take advantage of me".

"Who, me?" replied Morgan, "how could I, with a pitchfork in one hand and a small pig under my arm, a bucket in the other hand, and a goat on a lead?"

"Well," replied Megan, "you could always stick the pitchfork in the ground and tie the goat to it, and place the bucket over the small pig!"

## At the Bar

This guy walks into a bar in Cardiff with this really great shirt on. The barman goes,

"That's a nice shirt – where'd you get it, mate?" The man replies, "David Evans."

This second guy walks into the bar with really good trousers on and the barman says,

"Where'd you get the great trousers, butty?" The man replies, "David Evans."

This third guy walks into the bar with nice black suede shoes and yellow socks on. The barman goes, "Where'd you get the shoes and socks, butty?"

The man replies, "David Evans."

Then a fourth guy runs in naked and the barman goes, "Who the hell are you, mate?" And the naked guy says, "David Evans!"

\* \* \*

Two Irishmen met in a bar and one said to the other, "Have ye seen Mulligan lately, Mick?" Mick said, "Well, I have and I haven't."

"Well, what d'ye mean by that?" Mick said, "It's like this, y'see. I saw a chap who I thought was Mulligan, and he saw a chap that he thought was me. And when we got up to one another, it was neither of us."

\* \* \*

O'Riley sold Patrick a donkey; three weeks later they met in Murphy's pub and Patrick says, "Hi, O'Riley. That bloody donkey you sold me went and died." O'Riley just sipped his pint and chirped up, "By Jesus, it never done that on me!"

* * *

Ianto and Ifan, both slightly drunk, were walking home along the railway tracks one evening.

"There's a hell of a lot of steps here," says Ianto. Ifan says, "I'll tell you what's worse – this handrail is bloody low down!"

* * *

A tipsy Seamus gets on a bus in Ireland and asks the driver how long the trip is between Limerick and Cork. "About two hours," says the conductor.

"OK," says Seamus, "then how long is the trip between Cork and Limerick?" The irate driver says to him: "It's still about two hours. Why'd you think there'd be a difference?"

"Well," says Seamus, "it's only a week between Christmas and New Year, but it's a hell of a long time between New Year and Christmas!"

* * *

Ianto and Gerwyn were having a quiet pint in the Red, when a fire alarm went off. Ianto ran down the road.

"Hey," shouted Gerwyn, "I didn't know you were a fireman, Ianto!"

"I'm not," said Ianto, "but Myfanwy's husband is!"

* * *

The following was seen on a poster in Argyll:
    DRINK IS YOUR ENEMY.
Adjacent to this was another poster, which said:
    LOVE YOUR ENEMY.

* * *

In Scotland they have a new clinic for those who want to stop smoking. It's called Nicotines Anonymous. If you get the urge to smoke, you call them and they send a man over with a bottle of Scotch and you get drunk together.

* * *

Hamish was staggering home carrying a bottle of fine whisky when he slipped and fell heavily. Struggling to his feet, he felt something wet running down his leg. "Please, God," he implored, "let it be blood!"

* * *

Hamish was travelling in a train seated next to a stern-faced clergyman. As Hamish pulled out a bottle of whisky from his pocket the clergyman glared and said reprovingly, "Look here, I am sixty five and I have never tasted whisky in my life!"

"Dinna worry, Minister," smiled Hamish, pouring himself a dram. "There's no risk of you starting now!"

* * *

Jock was drinking at a pub all night. When he got up to leave, he fell flat on his face. He tried to stand again, but to no avail, falling flat on his face. He decided to crawl outside and get some fresh air to see whether that would sober him up. Once outside, he stood up and, sure enough, fell flat on his face. So, being a practical Scot, he crawled all the way home.

When he got to the door, he stood up yet again, but fell flat on his face. He crawled through the door into his bedroom. When he reached his bed, he tried once more to stand upright. This time he managed to pull himself to his feet but fell into bed. He was sound asleep as soon as his head hit the pillow.

He woke the next morning to his wife shaking him and shouting, "So Jock, ye've been oot drinkin' as usual!"

"Why would ye say that?" he complained innocently.

"Because the pub called an' ye left yer wheelchair there again!"

* * *

Jock and Rob had been drinking buddies and friends for years. After having a few drinks in a bar, Jock said to Rob, "We have been friends for years and years and if I should die before you do, would you do me a big favour? Get the best bottle of Scottish whisky you can find and pour it over my grave." Rob replied, "I would be glad to do that for you my old friend. But would you mind if I filtered it through ma kidneys first?"

* * *

Wee Sandy once attended a temperance lecture given by Scotland's top medical man, a noted anti-drink campaigner. The speaker began by placing a live, wriggling worm in a glass of whisky. After a moment or two it died and sank to the bottom.

The speaker said quietly to the audience, "Now my friends, what does this tell us?"
Sandy piped up, "If you drink whisky you'll not be bothered by worms!"

* * *

A drunk gets up from the bar and heads for the Gents. A few minutes later, a loud, blood-curdling scream is heard coming from the toilet.

A few minutes after that, another loud scream echos through the bar. The bartender goes into the Gents to investigate what the drunk is screaming about.

The bartender yells, "What's all the screaming about in there? You're scaring my customers!"

The drunk responds, "I'm just sitting here on the toilet and every time I try to flush, something comes up and squeezes the hell out of my balls." The bartender opens the door and looks in.

"You idiot! You're sitting on the mop bucket!"

* * *

An American walks into an Irish pub and says, "I'll give anyone £100 if they can drink ten pints of Guinness in ten minutes."

Most people just ignore the absurd bet and go back to their conversations. One guy even leaves the bar. A little while later that guy comes back and asks the American, "Is that bet still on?"

"Sure." So the bartender lines ten Guinnesses up on the bar. The Irishman drinks them all in less than ten minutes. As the American hands over the money, he asks, "Where did you go when you just left?" The Irishman answers, "I just went next door to the other pub to see if I could do it."

* * *

The local magistrate had given Dai a lecture on the evils of drink. But in view of the fact that this was the first time he had been drunk and incapable, the case was dismissed on payment of two pounds' costs.

"Now don't let me ever see your face again," said the Justice of the Peace sternly as the defendant turned to go.

"I'm afraid I can't promise that, sir," said Dai.

"And why not?"

"Because I'm the barman at your local!"

* * *

Angus walked into a bar, seriously drunk, and after staring for some time at the only lass seated at the bar, he walked over to her and kissed her. She jumped up and slapped him across the face. He immediately apologized and explained, "I'm sorry. I thought you were my missus. You look exactly like her."

"Why you worthless, insufferable, wretched, no-good drunk!" she screamed.

"Funny," muttered Angus, "you even sound exactly like her."

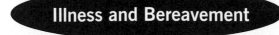

# Illness and Bereavement

Ianto was rushed into Bronglais hospital with a suspected leg fracture. A student doctor approached him with a syringe.

"What are you going to do with that?" asked Ianto, slightly alarmed.

"Don't worry," replied the student doctor. "It's only a little prick with a needle."

"I know that," said Ianto, "but I asked you what are you going to do with it."

\* \* \*

Old Hamish was on his deathbed. Tenderly, his wife Maggie knelt by his bedside and asked: "Anything I can get you, Hamish?" No reply.

"Have ye no' a last wish, Hamish?" Faintly came the answer, "a wee bit of yon boiled ham, my dearie."

"Och, man," said Maggie. "Ye ken no have that – it's for the funeral."

\* \* \*

Ianto calls the hospital. He says, "You've got to send help! My wife's having a baby!" The nurse says, "Calm down. Is this her first child?" Ianto replied, "No! This is her bloody husband!"

\* \* \*

Liam opened the morning newspaper and was dumbfounded to read in the obituary column that he had died. He quickly phoned his best friend, Tony.

"Did you see the paper?" asked Liam. "They say I died!"
"Yes, I saw it!" replied Tony. "Where are you calling from?"

* * *

Hamish had been admitted to Aberdeen Infirmary with dysentery upon returning from an African safari trip. He had spent three miserable days on a liquid diet trying to recuperate, and smiling as best he could while visitors stopped in to wish him well and hope he didn't have an attack of diarrhoea. The nurse knocked on his door, peeked in, and informed him that he had more visitors on the way up. He prepared himself for the visit, when a sudden onslaught of diarrhoea caught him by surprise, making a mess of his hospital gown and bed sheets. Not wanting to be embarrassed when his visitors showed up, he quickly took off his hospital gown, ripped the sheets off the bed, and threw them out the window, and quickly ran into his bathroom to clean up and put on another hospital gown.

Unbeknown to Hamish, Angus McDuff had just left the local pub and was staggering along the street below his window, when the hospital gown and sheets fell on top of him. Assuming he had been attacked, Angus turned around, covered by the sheets, swinging blindly and punching out at his 'attacker'. When he finally managed to knock the sheets off, he fell backwards on his backside and sat up staring at the pile of sheets in awe. Just then, the local bobby turned up. Trying to comprehend the sight before him, he asked Angus, "and just what in the hell happened here?" Angus replied, "I don't know, sir; but, I think I just beat the shit out of a ghost!"

* * *

Mary O'Reilly was standing vigil over her husband Patrick's deathbed. As she held his hand, her warm tears ran silently down her face, splashed onto his face, and roused him from his slumber. He looked up and his pale lips began to move slightly.

"My darlin' Mary," he whispered.

"Hush, my love," she said. "Go back to sleep. Shhh, don't talk." But he was insistent.

"Mary," he said in his tired voice. "I have to talk. I have something I must confess to you."

"There's nothing to confess," replied the weeping Mary. "It's all right. Everything's all right, go to sleep now."

"No, no. I must die in peace, Mary. I slept with your two sisters, your best friend Kathleen, and your mother." Mary mustered a pained smile and stroked his hand. "Hush now Patrick, don't torment yourself. I know all about it," she said. "Why do you think I poisoned you?"

* * *

Patrick, who was eighty-eight years old, had been feeling quite ill during the past few months. One day his son Seamus persuaded him to see his doctor. After a complete examination at the surgery, the doctor spoke to Patrick and Seamus in his office. "I've got bad news for you, Patrick. Your heart's near given out and you've only two months to live." Patrick was stunned but after a few minutes he turns to Seamus and says, "I've had a good long life, and if the good Lord wants me then I've got no complaints. Let's be off to the pub where I'm after having a few pints with my friends." When they got to the pub a few of Patrick's old cronies see him.

"Ah, Paddy – how're you feeling today?" says one.

"Not good, Liam. The doctor has told me I've two months to live."

"What a shame," says Liam. "And what's the problem"?

"The doctor says I have AIDS." After a few moments Seamus gets his father alone and says, "Hey, Dad. It's not AIDS you've got; it's a heart condition."

"Sure, don't I know that – I just don't want them old buggers trying to sleep with your ma when I'm gone."

\* \* \*

Jock's wife Maggie went to the doctor complaining of pains in the stomach. The doctor told her it was 'just wind'.

"Just wind?" she screamed at him. "It was just wind that blew down the Tay Bridge!"

\* \* \*

Dai goes to the family doctor and asks if he can have a vasectomy. The doctor asks him if he's discussed the matter with his family.

"Of course," replied Dai, "and they're all in favour, 15 to 1!"

\* \* \*

Doctor Kildare finished his examination and told old Donald to come into his surgery.

"Sit down, Donald. After looking at these results, I recommend that you should have an operation immediately." Donald thought for a long moment. "Doctor, how will this affect my hobby?"

"What's your hobby, Donald?"

"Saving money!"

\* \* \*

Mrs Gethin was looking for the grave of her late husband – a notorious swindler – as it has been quite a while since she was there last. She went to the Council office and said, "I am looking for my husband's grave."

"OK, madam," said the officer. "What was his name?"

"Gareth Gethin," she answers. He looks through his large book for quite a time and says, "I'm sorry, there are no Gareth Gethins in our cemetery; in fact there's only one Gethin registered: a Mary Gethin". The woman brightens up and says, "Of course, that's it; everything was in my name".

\* \* \*

Raymond walks past a mental hospital in Welshpool, and hears a moaning voice, "Thirteen, thirteen, thirteen, thirteen..." He looks at the hospital and sees a hole in the wall. He looks through the hole and gets poked in the eye. The moaning voice then continues to moan, "Fourteen, fourteen, fourteen, fourteen…"

* * *

Ianto asks the doctor, "Can you give me the bad news first?" The doctor replies, "You've got AIDS."

"Oh, no! What could be worse than that?" asks Ianto.

"You've also got Alzheimer's Disease."

Looking relieved Ianto says, "Oh, well. That's not so bad – at least I don't have AIDS."

* * *

Geraint and Olwen – both 80 years old – were having problems remembering things, so they decided to go to their doctor to get checked out, to make sure nothing was wrong with them. When they arrived at the surgery, they explained to the doctor about the problems they were having with their memory. After checking the couple out, the doctor told them that they were physically okay but might want to start writing things down and make notes to help them remember things.

They both thanked the doctor and left. Later that night while watching TV, Geraint got up from his chair.

"Where are you going?" Olwen asked.

"To the kitchen," he replied.

"Will you get me a bowl of ice cream?"

"Certainly."

"Don't you think you should write it down so you can remember it?"

"No, I can remember that."

"Well, I would also like some strawberries on top. You had better write that down because I know you'll forget that."

"I can remember that. You want a bowl of ice cream with strawberries."

"Well I also would like whipped cream on top. I know you will forget that so you better write it down."

With irritation in his voice, Geraint said, "I don't need to write that down! I can remember that." He then fumed into the kitchen. After about twenty minutes, he returned from the kitchen and handed her a plate of bacon and eggs. Olwen stared at the plate for a moment and said angrily: "I told you to write it down! You forgot my toast!"

* * *

Marie accompanied her husband Ianto to the doctor's surgery. After his check-up, the doctor called Marie into his office alone. He said, "Ianto is suffering from a very severe disease, combined with chronic stress. If you don't do the following, Ianto will surely die.

"Each morning, fix him a healthy breakfast. Be pleasant, and make sure he is in a good mood. For lunch make him a nutritious meal. For dinner prepare an especially nice meal for him. Don't burden him with housework, as he probably has had a hard day. Don't discuss your problems with him; it will only make his stress worse. And most importantly, make love with your husband several times a week and satisfy his every whim. If you can do this for the next ten months to a year, I think Ianto will be a new man and will regain his health completely."

On the way home, Ianto asked his Marie, "What did the doctor say?"

"You're going to die," Marie replied.

* * *

Beryl goes to the doctor's office and says, "Doctor Jones, I've got an awfully embarrassing problem… I can't stop farting. They don't make a sound and they don't even smell, but I just can't stop. In fact, I've farted four times just since I've been in your surgery!" Puzzled, Doctor Jones begins to examine Beryl. He listens to her breathing, checks her sinuses and blood pressure, looks at her throat and then sits down at his desk.

"Well," he says, "I'm glad that you came to see me when you did. Here are some pills. I want you take one twice a day. Come back in a week to let me know how you're doing." Beryl thanked the doctor and left, then she returns a week later.

"Doctor Jones, those pills didn't work at all – in fact, they made things worse! I'm still farting just as often, but now they really stink!" The doctor said, "Well, it looks like we've got your sinuses sorted out. Now we can work on your hearing."

* * *

More and more doctors are running their practices like an assembly line. Mickey walked into a doctor's surgery and the receptionist asked him what he had. Mickey replied, "Piles". So she took down his name, address, and medical insurance number and told him to be seated. Fifteen minutes later a nurse's aide came out and asked Mickey what he had.

"The piles," he replied. So she took down his height, weight, a complete medical history and told him to wait in the examining room. A half-hour later a nurse came in and asked Mickey again what he had.

"Piles," he said again. She gave him a blood test, a blood pressure test, an electrocardiogram, told him to take off all his clothes and wait for the doctor. An hour later the doctor came in and asked Mickey what he had. "I have the piles, Doctor."

"Where?"

"Outside in the truck. Where do you want them?"

# Religion

Patrick, feeling guilty about his relationship with a girl, was encouraged by his friend Murphy to go to Church to confess. He went into the confession booth and told the priest, "Father O'Reilly, I have sinned. I have committed fornication with a young lady. Please forgive me."

Father O'Reilly said, "Tell me who the young girl was." Patrick said he couldn't do that and Father O'Reilly said he couldn't grant him forgiveness unless he did.

"Was it Mollie O'Grady?" asked Father O'Reilly."

"No."

"Was it Rosie Kelly?"

"No."

"Was it that red-headed wench Tessie O'Malley?"

"No."

"Well then," said Father O'Reilly, "you'll not be forgiven."

When Patrick met Murphy outside, Murphy asked him, "So, did you find forgiveness?"

"No," said Patrick, "but I picked up three good leads!"

* * *

Pat and Mike were doing some street repairs in front of a known house of ill repute in Boston. A Jewish Rabbi came walking down the street, looked left, looked right, and ducked into the house. Pat paused a bit from swinging his pickaxe and said, "Mike, will you look at that! A man of the cloth, and going into a place like that in broad daylight!" A bit later, a Baptist minister came down the street, looked to the left, looked to the right, and scurried into the house. Mike laid down his shovel, turned to Pat and said, "Pat! Are you seeing what I'm seeing? A man of the Church, and he's giving that place his custom!"

Just then, a Catholic Priest came down the street, looked to the left, looked to the right, and slipped into the bawdy house. Pat and Mike straightened up, removed their hats, and Mike says, "Faith, and there must be somebody sick in there."

* * *

Father Michael walks into a pub in Donegal, and says to the first man he meets, "Do you want to go to heaven?" The man said, "I do, Father." The priest replied, "Then stand over there against the wall." Then the priest asked the second man, "Do you want to go to heaven?"

"Certainly, Father," was the man's reply.

"Then stand over there against the wall," said the priest. Then Father Michael walked up to O'Riley and said, "Do you want to go to heaven?"

O'Riley said, "No, I don't, Father." The priest said, "I don't believe this. You mean to tell me that when you die you don't want to go to heaven?" O'Riley said, "Oh, when I die, yes. I thought you were getting a group together to go right now."

* * *

Father Michael was warning his listeners about the suddenness of death. "Before another day is ended," he thundered, "somebody in this parish will die". Seated in the front row was a little old Irishman who laughed out loud at this statement. Very angry, Father Michael said to the jovial old man, "What's so funny?"

"Well," spoke up the old feller, "I'm not a member of this parish."

* * *

Father O'Rourke, the new priest is nervous about hearing confessions, so he asks the older father to sit in on his sessions. O'Rourke hears a couple of confessions, then the old priest asks him to step out of the confessional for a few suggestions.

"First," the old priest suggests, "cross your arms over your chest, and rub your chin with one hand." Father O'Rourke tries this.

"Now try saying things like, 'I see… yes, go on. I understand,' and 'how did you feel about that?'"

Father O'Rourke says those things.

"Now," says the old priest, "don't you think that's a little better than slapping your knee and saying 'No shit! What happened next?'"

\* \* \*

Mick is lying in bed, very ill. His son is sitting at his bedside, expecting the end to come at any moment. Mick looks up at his son and says, "Son, it's time for you to get me a Protestant minister." His son is astounded.

"But Dad!" he protests, "You've been a good Catholic all your life! You're delirious. It's a priest you need now, not a minister." Mick looks up at him and says, "Son, please. It's my last request. Get a minister for me!"

"But Dad," cries the son, "you raised me a good Catholic. You've been a good Catholic all your life. You don't want a minister at a time like this!"

Mick manages to croak out the words, "Son, if you respect me and love me as a father, you'll go out and get me a Protestant minister right now." The son relents and goes out and gets the minister. They come back to the house, and the minister goes upstairs and converts him. As the minister is leaving the house, he passes Father O'Shea coming quickly through the door. The minister stares solemnly into the eyes of the priest:

"I'm afraid you're too late, Father," he says. "He's a Protestant now." Father O'Shea rushes up the steps and bursts into Mick's room.

"Mick! Mick! Why did you do it?" he cries. "You were such a good Catholic! We went to St. Mary's together! You were there when I performed my first mass! Why in the world would you do such a thing like this?"

"Well," Mick says as he looks up at his dear friend, "I figured if somebody had to go, it was better one of them than one of us."

* * *

One little atheist boy's parents were very concerned about his grades in school. They noticed that his study habits were poor, that he wouldn't concentrate, and that he had zero initiative as far as homework was concerned, so they decided to send him to a Catholic school. They noticed an immediate improvement in his overall school performance, especially in maths. Every day he would come home from school and promptly head upstairs and begin studying his numbers. Amazed, his parents asked him what it was that motivated him to study so hard.

"Is it that the nuns are so strict with you getting your schoolwork finished?" they asked.

"No," said the boy.

"Is it that the subjects they are giving you are challenging to you?"

"No." responded the boy.

"What is it, then, that makes you so eager to study at this new school?" they queried.

"Well," said the boy, "my very first day of school at Our Lady of Perpetual Motion, I was sitting in class, looking around and not paying much attention. Then I looked up and saw this naked guy nailed to a plus sign, and I figured they must mean business!"

* * *

Sister Brigid was teaching her young students one day and she asked each of them what they would like to be when they grew up. She came to a little girl who responded, "When I grow up I want to be a prostitute." Shocked, good Sister Brigid fainted on the spot. Her students rushed to revive her. When she came around, Sister asked the little girl, "What did you say you wanted to be when you grew up?" The little girl replied, "A prostitute."

"Oh, thank goodness," the relieved nun replied. "I thought you said a Protestant."

\* \* \*

A Catholic priest is driving down to Dublin and gets stopped by the garda for speeding. The officer smells alcohol on the priest's breath and then sees an empty wine bottle on the floor of the car. He says, "Sir, have you been drinking?"

"Just water," says the priest. The officer says, "Then why do I smell wine?" The priest looks at the bottle and says, "Be Jesus! Another miracle!"

\* \* \*

The reverend Harri Parri is seated next to a rabbi on a flight from Cardiff to Heathrow.

The flight attendant asks the preacher, "Cocktail, sir?" Infuriated, the good preacher responds, "I'd sooner commit adultery."

She asks the rabbi, "How about you, sir?" Rabbi responds, "I'll have what he's having."

\* \* \*

The Methodist minister was sharing a rail compartment with Goronwy who was rather drunk, and insisted on talking.

"Please don't speak to me," said the minister. "You're drunk."

"Drunk?" replied Goronwy. "You're worse than me – you've got your collar on back to front!"

* * *

Dai stumbled out of the Red Cow right into the arms of Mr Jones, a Wesleyan minister.

"Drunk again!" declared the preacher. "Shame on you! When are you going to straighten out your life?"

"Mr Jones," asked Dai. "What causes arthritis?"

"I'll tell you what causes it! Drinking cheap beer, gambling and carousing around with loose women. How long have you had arthritis?"

"I don't," slurred Dai. "The Bishop has it!"

* * *

A wealthy farmer from Llanbrynmair went to chapel one Sunday. After services he said to the preacher, "Mr Jones, that was a damned good sermon you gave, damned good!"

"I'm happy you liked it," said the preacher. "But I wish you wouldn't use those terms in expressing yourself."

"I can't help it," said the rich farmer. "I still think it was a damned good sermon. In fact, I liked it so much I put a fifty pound note in the collection basket."

"Bloody hell, that was good of you!" replied the preacher.

* * *

A Canton priest and a Grangetown rabbi found themselves sharing a compartment on the train to Barry Island. After a while, the priest struck up a conversation by saying, "I know that in your religion, you're not supposed to eat pork. Have you actually ever tasted it?"

"I must tell the truth," the rabbi said. "Yes, I have, on the odd occasion." Then it was the rabbi's turn to interrogate. He asked, "And in your religion… I know you're supposed to be celibate. But have you ever…?"

"Yes, I know what you're going to ask," said the priest, "and I confess that I have succumbed once or twice." There was silence for a while. Then the rabbi peeped around the newspaper he was reading and said, "Better than pork, isn't it?"

* * *

Dai, Ianto and Evan were talking about death and dying: "When you're in the casket and your mates and family are mourning you, what would you like to hear them say about you?" asks Evan.

"I would like to hear them say that I was a great doctor of my time and a great family man," says Dai.

"I would like to hear that I was a wonderful husband and school teacher who made a huge difference for our children," says Ianto.

Evan says, "I would like to hear them say, 'Look, he's moving!'"

* * *

As soon as she had finished convent school, a bright young girl named Laura shook the dust of Ireland off her shoes and made her way to New York, where she became successful in show business. Eventually she returned home for a visit, and on the Saturday night went to confession in her old church, which she had attended as a young child. In the confessional, the priest recognized her and began asking her about her work. She explained that she was an acrobatic dancer, and he wanted to know what that meant. She said she would be happy to show him the kind of thing she did on stage. She stepped out of the box and within sight of the priest she went into a series of cartwheels, leaping splits, handsprings and backflips.

Kneeling near the confessional, waiting their turn, were two middle-aged ladies. They witnessed Laura's acrobatics with wide eyes, and one said to the other: "Will you just look at the penance the priest is giving out tonight, and I haven't even got my knickers on!"

* * *

Iwan, Evan and Dai are invited to a Christmas Eve party at the White Lion, and they are told to bring something with a

Christmas theme. They find themselves at the door waiting to go in. Iwan searches his pocket, and finds some mistletoe, and he is allowed in. Evan presents a cracker, and he is also allowed in.

Dai pulls out a pair of panties. Confused at this last offering, the landlord of the White Lion asks, "How do these represent Christmas?" Dai responds: "They're Carol's."

\* \* \*

Ifan asked his dad if he could borrow the car and his dad replied, "No, not until you cut your hair!"

"But dad, Jesus had long hair!" said Ifan.

"Yeah, but Jesus walked everywhere," said his dad.

\* \* \*

The preacher shocked the congregation when he announced that he was resigning from the chapel and moving to a nicer part of Wales. After the service, a very distraught lady came to the preacher with tears in her eyes, "Oh, Mr Jones, we are going to miss you so much. We don't want you to leave!" The kind-hearted preacher patted her hand and said, "Now, now, Megan fach, don't carry on. The new preacher who takes my place might be even better than me".

"Yes, Mr Jones," she said, her voice full of disappointment. "That's what they said last time, too…"

\* \* \*

One afternoon little Dafydd was playing outdoors. He used his mother's broom as a horse and had a wonderful time until it was getting dark. He left the broom on the back porch. His mother was cleaning up the kitchen when she realized that her broom was missing. She asked Dafydd about the broom and he told her where it was. She then asked Dafydd bach to please go get it. Dafydd told his mam that he was afraid of the dark and didn't want to go out to get the broom. His mam smiled and said, "God is out there too, so don't be afraid". Dafydd opened the back door a little and said, "God if you're out there, can you pass me the broom please?"

\* \* \*

A minister dies, and when he gets to heaven, he sees a Llanwrtyd Wells taxi driver who has more crowns. He says to an angel, "I don't understand. I devoted my whole life to my congregation."

"We reward results," the angel says. "Did your congregation always pay attention when you gave a sermon?"

"Once in a while someone fell asleep," says the preacher.

"Right. But when people rode in this fellow's taxi, they not only stayed awake, but they usually prayed!"

\* \* \*

Myfanwy goes to confession one morning and says to the priest, "Forgive me, father, but I have sinned."

"What have you done, my child?" enquires the priest.

"Every morning when I wake up," replied Myfanwy, "I look into the mirror and tell myself how beautiful I am."

"My dear," said the priest, "go away and rejoice. That's no sin, that's just a mistake."

\* \* \*

One Sunday morning, the preacher noticed that Tomi bach was staring up at the large plaque that hung in the church foyer. It was covered with names. The seven-year-old had been staring at the plaque for some time, so the preacher walked up, stood beside Tomi, and said quietly, "Good morning, Tomi bach, and how are you today?"

"Oh, good morning, Mr Jones," replied Tomi, still focused on the plaque. "Can you tell me what this is?"

"Well, Tomi, it's a memorial to all the young men and women who died in the service." Soberly, they stood together, staring at the large plaque. Little Johnny's voice was barely audible when he asked, "Which service, the morning or the evening?"

## Eating Out

Evan and Gomer went into a posh cafe and ordered two teas. They then took out their sandwiches from their sandwich boxes and started to eat. The waiter noticed this and became quite indignant. He marched over and told them, "You can't eat your own sandwiches in here!" Evan looked at Gomer, they both shrugged their shoulders and then swapped sandwiches.

\* \* \*

Sian was a woman who had a maddening passion for baked beans. She loved them, but unfortunately they had always had a very embarrassing and somewhat lively reaction to her. Then one day, she met Dafydd and fell in love. When it became apparent that they would marry, she thought to herself, "He is such a sweet and gentle man, he would never go for this carrying on." So she made the supreme sacrifice and gave up beans.

Some months later her car broke down on the way home from work. Since she lived in the country, she called Dafydd and told him that she would be late because she had to walk home. On her way, she passed a cafe and the smell of the baked beans was more than she could stand. Since she still had miles to walk, she figured that she would walk off any ill effects by the time she reached home. So, she stopped at the cafe and before she knew it, she had eaten three large plates of baked beans on toast. All the way home she putt-putted, and upon arriving home she felt reasonably sure she could control it.

Dafydd was excited to see her and exclaimed delightedly,

"Cariad, I have a surprise for dinner tonight." He then blindfolded her and led her to her chair at the table. She seated herself and just as he was about to remove her blindfold, the telephone rang. He made her promise not to touch the blindfold until he returned. He then went to answer the telephone. The baked beans she had consumed were still affecting her and the pressure was becoming almost unbearable, so while Dafydd was out of the room she seized the opportunity, shifted her weight to one leg and let it go. It was not only loud, but it smelled like a fish lorry running over a dead pig in front of a sewage works. She took her napkin and fanned the air around her vigorously. Then, she shifted to the other cheek and ripped three more, which reminded her of cooked cabbage. Keeping her ears tuned to the conversation in the other room, she went on like this for another ten minutes. When the telephone farewells were given, it told her that the end of her freedom had come, she fanned the air a few more times with her napkin, placed it on her lap and folded her hands upon it, smiling contentedly to herself. She was the picture of innocence when Dafydd returned, apologizing for taking so long, he asked her if she peeked and she assured him that she had not. At this point, he removed the blindfold, and good lord, was she surprised – there were twelve dinner guests seated around the table to wish her a happy birthday!

* * *

Customer: Give me a Glamorgan Sausage.
Waiter: With pleasure.
Customer: No, with mustard.

* * *

A man from Adamstown went into a deli in Cardiff city centre and took a seat at the lunch counter. "A corned beef sandwich," he ordered.

"Corned beef sandwich is not on the menu, but I can give you a sandwich with corned beef in it, like our Midnight Special."

"What's a Midnight Special?"

"A triple decker with corned beef, tongue, bologna, tomato, lettuce, onion, pickle and mayonnaise, on toasted raisin bread."

"Could you just place a piece of corned beef between two slices of white bread and serve it to me on a plate?"

"Why, sure!" Then, turning to the sandwich man, he sang out: "One Midnight Special. Make it one deck, hold the tongue, bologna, tomato, lettuce, onion, pickle and mayonnaise, and make the raisin bread white, untoasted!"

\* \* \*

At an exclusive restaurant in Cardiff Bay, a waiter brings the customer his 12oz steak, with his thumb over the meat.

"Excuse me!" said the customer. "Your hand is on my steak!"

"What?" answers the waiter. "You don't want it to fall on the floor again, surely?"

\* \* \*

Same restaurant, same waiter, serving two gentlemen at a table: "Tea or coffee, gentlemen?"

"I'll have tea."

"Me, too – and be sure the glass is clean!"

The waiter exits, and returns shortly with the teas.

"Two teas! Which of you asked for the clean glass?"

Sport

How do we know that golf was invented in Scotland? Well, the whole point of the game is to hit the ball as few times as possible in the course of a round, and any Scotsman can tell you that the fewer times you hit a ball, the longer it will last.

\* \* \*

The river warden catches Aled leaving the vicinity of the Nant Hir reservoir with a bucket of fish.

"Aha! I've caught you poaching fish red-handed," says the warden.

"What do you mean, red-handed?" says Aled.

"You've got a bucket full of fish right there. You can't talk your way out of it this time."

"Oh, come off it," says Aled, "I've not poached a single fish – these are my pets. I bring them to the reservoir once a week for exercise. After they've had a good swim, they come back to the bucket and we go home together."

"Do you expect me to believe that?"

"I can prove it," says Aled.

So they walk back to the reservoir and Aled dips the bucket in and the fish swim away. They stand in silence as the minutes tick by… one minute, five minutes, ten minutes… No sign of the fish coming back to the pail.

"Ah, you lying scoundrel! shouts the warden. "Where are your fish?"

"Fish? What fish?"

Alan and Tony were out playing golf in Borth, neither taking it particularly seriously. Dangerously over par, they approach the 18th. Alan, starting to line his ball up on the tee just so, takes some pretty impressive practice swings and checks the wind direction. Tony asks, "What are you doing? You haven't taken this seriously all day". Alan, now peering intently into the distance towards the flag replies, "My wife's in the clubhouse". He continues with his fussing until Tony says, "Look, I don't care how much you line that ball up – you'll never hit her from here!"

* * *

Cyril and Andy are playing golf on a course that is right next to a cemetery. After they tee off, Andy notices that there is a funeral procession passing by. So he takes off his hat, and places it over his heart. When the funeral is over, Cyril looks at Andy and asks, "Why did you do that?"

"It's the least I could do," Andy replies. "We were married for almost 40 years."

* * *

Murphy got home from his Sunday round of golf later than normal and very tired. "Bad day at the course?" his wife asked.

"Everything was going fine," he said. "Then Patrick had a heart attack and died on the tenth tee."

"Oh, that's awful!"

"You're not kidding. For the whole back nine it was hit the ball, drag Patrick, hit the ball, drag Patrick…"

* * *

Liam is stranded on a desert island, all alone for ten years. One day, he sees a speck in the horizon. He thinks to himself, "It's not a ship." The speck gets a little closer and he thinks, "It's not a boat." The speck gets even closer and he thinks, "It's not a raft." Then, out of the surf comes this beautiful, voluptuous blonde woman, wearing a wet suit and scuba gear. She comes up to Liam and says, "How long has it been since you've had a cigarette?"

"Ten years!" Liam replies.

She reaches over and unzips a waterproof pocket on her left sleeve and pulls out a pack of fresh cigarettes. He takes one, lights it, takes a long drag, and says, "Bejesus! Is that good?"

Then she asked, "How long has it been since you've had a drink of whiskey?" Liam replies, "Ten years!" She reaches over, unzips her waterproof pocket on her right sleeve, pulls out a flask and gives it to him. He takes a long swig and says, "Wow, bejesus, that's fantastic!"

Then she starts unzipping a longer zipper that runs down the front of her wet suit and she says to him, "And how long has it been since you've had some real fun?" And Liam replies, "Bejesus! Don't tell me that you've a dart board in there!"

* * *

A couple of old Dubliners were golfing when one said he was going to Dr Taylor for a new set of dentures in the morning. His friend remarked that he had gone to the same dentist a few years before.

"Is that so?" the first said. "Did he do a good job?"

"Well, I was on the course yesterday when the fellow on the ninth hole hooked a shot," he said. "The ball must have been going 200 mph when it hit me in the goolies. That," he added, "bejesus, was the first time in two years my teeth didn't hurt."

* * *

After a particularly poor game of golf, a popular club member skipped the clubhouse and started to go home. As he was walking to the parking lot to get his car, a policeman stopped him and asked, "Did you tee off on the sixteenth hole about twenty minutes ago?"

"Yes," the golfer responded.

"Did you happen to hook your ball so that it went over the trees and off the course?"

"Yes, I did. How did you know?" he asked.

"Well," said the policeman very seriously, "Your ball flew out onto the highway and crashed through a driver's windshield. The car went out of control, crashing into five other cars and a fire truck. The fire truck couldn't make it to the fire, and the building burned down. So, what are you going to do about it?"

The golfer thought it over carefully and responded. "I think I'll close my stance a little bit, tighten my grip and lower my right thumb."

* * *

Tickets for the British Open soon to be held at the Celtic Manor resort are hard to get and the touts have a field day offering tickets in advance for £50.

"That's absurd," Maldwyn commented. "Why, I could get a woman for that!"

"True sir, but with this ticket you get eighteen holes!"

* * *

Robert, who was also an avid golfer, found himself with a few hours to spare one afternoon on the Royal and Ancient. He figured if he hurried and played very fast, he could get in nine holes before he had to head home. Just as he was about to tee off, an old gentleman shuffled onto the tee and asked if he could accompany the young man as he was golfing alone. Not being able to say no, he allowed the old gent to join him.

To his surprise the old man played fairly quickly. He didn't hit the ball far, but plodded along consistently and didn't waste much time. Finally, they reached the ninth fairway and Robert found himself with a tough shot. There was a large pine tree right in front of his ball – and directly between his ball and the green.

After several minutes of debating how to hit the shot the old man finally said, "You know, when I was your age I'd hit the ball right over that tree." With that challenge placed before him, Robert swung hard, hit the ball up, right smack into the top of the tree trunk and it thudded back on the ground not a foot from where it had originally lay.

The old man offered one more comment: "Of course, when I was your age that pine tree was only three feet tall."

\* \* \*

A couple of women were playing golf one sunny Saturday morning at Borth and Ynyslas. The first of the twosome teed off and watched in horror as her ball headed directly toward a foursome of men playing up the eighteenth hole. Indeed, the ball hit Ianto, and he immediately clasped his hands together at his crotch, fell to the ground and proceeded to roll around in evident agony. The woman rushed down to Ianto and immediately began to apologize. She explained that she was a physical therapist: "Please allow me to help. I know I could relieve your pain if you'd allow me," she told him earnestly.

"Ummph, oooh, nnooo, I'll be alright. I'll be fine in a few minutes," replied Ianto breathlessly as he remained in the fetal position still clasping his hands together at his crotch. But she persisted, and Ianto finally allowed her to help him. She gently took his hands away and laid them to the side, she loosened his pants, and she put her hands inside. She began to massage him. She then asked him: "How does that feel?" To which Ianto replied: "It feels bloody great, but my thumb still hurts like hell."

\* \* \*

Hamish joined a threesome; and as he'd had a very successful day he was invited back the next day for a game at 8 a.m. "Look fellers, I'd sure like to play," said Hamish, "but I could be two minutes late!"

Next morning he showed up right on time and played another

lovely round, but this time he played every stroke left-handed. Again, he was invited to join the threesome at 8 a.m. the following day.

"Sure, I'll be here," said Hamish, "but remember I could be late; if so, it will only be a couple of minutes!"

"We'll wait," one of the golfers assured him. "But by the way, could you explain something that's been mystifying us all? Yesterday you played right-handed and today you played left-handed. Obviously you're proficient at both, so how do you decide which way to play?"

"Ah well," Hamish answered, "when I wake up in the morning, if my darling wife's lying on her right side, I play right-handed and if she's lying on her left side, I play left-handed. Simple as that."

"But what if she's lying on her back?"

"Och, that's when I'm two minutes late!"

* * *

An Irishman and a Scotsman were talking about playing golf during the various seasons of the year.

"In most parts of Scotland we cannot play in the winter time. We have to wait until spring," the Scotsman said.

"Why, in Ireland we can even play in the winter time. Snow and cold are no object to us," said the Irishman.

"Well, what do you do – paint your balls black?" asked the Scotsman.

"No," said the Irishman, "we just put on an extra sweater or two."

* * *

Dai is waiting to tee off for the start of his round when he sees Will just finishing his round. Dai couldn't help but notice that Will is wet all over the front of his trousers. Curiosity gets the best of him, so Dai asks Will how he got so wet. Will tells the following story: that day, he had played golf for the first time with bifocals. All day long, he could see two sizes for everything. There was a big club and a little club; a big ball and a little ball; and so on. Therefore, Will said that he hit the little ball with the big club and it went straight and long all day long. On the green, he putted the little ball into the big cup. He said that he played the best golf of his life. Dai said, "I understand that, but how did you get all wet?"

"Well," said Will, "when I got to the 16th, I had to have a leak awfully bad. I went into the woods and unzipped my fly. When I looked down, there were two of them also; a big one and a little one. Well, I knew the big one wasn't mine, so I put it back."

* * *

Four caddies were caddying for a golfer around Llanrhystud Golf Course. His friends asked him why he had so many caddies.

"It was my wife's idea," he replied. "She thinks I should be spending more time with the kids."

* * *

Ianto goes on holiday to Cyprus and falls in love with a beautiful girl from the Rhondda fach. They spend the whole week together, and both are so infatuated with each other, they discuss the continuation of their relationship.

"Well" said Ianto, "I suppose it's only fair to tell you that I'm a golf fanatic. I live, eat and sleep golf."

"In that case," said Mair, "I'll be honest with you, and confess to being a hooker."

"Oh! That's no problem," said Ianto, "It's probably because you're not keeping your wrists together when you hold the club."

* * *

Angus goes to the doctor and says, "Doctor, I've got a cricket ball stuck up my behind."

"Have you indeed?" says the Doctor. "How's that?"

"Oh, don't you bloody start," says Angus.

* * *

Dai and Blodwen went on a fishing holiday resort up the north of Scotland. Dai liked to fish at the crack of dawn. Blodwen liked to read.

One morning Dai returned after several hours of fishing and decided to take a short nap. Although Blodwen wasn't familiar with the lake, she decided to take the boat, and rowed out a short distance, anchored, and returned to reading her book. Along came the bailiff in his boat. He pulled up alongside her and said, "Good morning, lass. What are you doing?"

"Reading my book," Blodwen replied.

"You're in a restricted fishing area," he informed her.

"But sir, I'm not fishing. Can't you see that?"

"Yes, but you have all the equipment. I'll have to take you in and charge you."

"If you do that, I'll have to charge you with rape," snapped an angry Blodwen.

"But I haven't even touched you," groused the bailiff.

"Yes, that's true," Blodwen replied, "but you have all the equipment."

# Tourists

A Texan rancher comes to Ireland and meets Liam, a farmer from County Wexford. The Texan says, "Takes me a whole goddam day to drive from one side of my ranch to the other." Liam replied, "Ah sure, I know, sir. I used to have a tractor like that once."

\* \* \*

A Texan and an Irishman were enjoying a ride in the country when they came upon an unusual sight – an old gallows. The American turned to his Irish travelling companion: "You see that, I reckon," said he to the Irishman, pointing to the gallows. "And now where would you be if the gallows had its due?"

"Riding alone," coolly replied Paddy.

\* \* \*

A Texan visiting Dublin said to O'Shea, "Back in the States we can erect a block of skyscrapers larger than them there in about two weeks. O'Shea replied, "We can start a row of houses in the morning and on the way home from work the bailiffs will be putting the tenants out for being behind with the rent."

\* \* \*

Patrick was proudly showing an American some Irish marrows in his allotment. The American said that in the States they had gherkins as big as marrows. Then Patrick showed him some cabbages. the American said that in the States they had brussel sprouts that size and that American cabbages were about three feet in diameter. Eventually the American pointed to some old gasometers and asked what they were. Patrick replied, "They're saucepans for cooking American cabbages".

* * *

Murphy was in New York. He was patiently waiting, and he was watching the traffic cop on a busy street crossing. The cop stopped the flow of traffic and shouted, "Okay, pedestrians". Then he'd allow the traffic to pass. He'd done this several times, and Murphy still stood on the sidewalk. After the cop had shouted "Pedestrians" for the tenth time, Murphy went over to him and said, "Is it not about time ye let the Catholics across?"

* * *

An American Protestant gets in a drinking contest in Ireland and, of course, loses. Later, he staggers into the local church and heads for the confession booth. The priest waits for the guy to start talking and waits. Finally the priest gently raps on the wall, and the guy responds, "We're both out of luck, buddy. There's no paper here either."

* * *

An Irish farmer was in his field digging up his spuds. An American farmer looked over the fence and said, "In Texas we grow potatoes five times larger than that!" The Irishman replied, "Ah, but we just grow them for our own mouths!"

* * *

Tourist in the Highlands: I'm sorry, waiter, but I only have enough money for the bill. I have nothing left for a tip.
Highland Waiter: Let me add up that bill again, sir.

* * *

A woman and a man from Aberdeen were stranded on a desert island after a shipwreck. Their clothes were in rags and their food running out.

"I suppose it could always be worse," said the woman.

"Oh aye, it could," agreed the Aberdonian. "I might have bought a return ticket."

* * *

Sandy was in London wearing his tartan when a curious lady asked if there was anything worn under the kilt.

"No, madam," he replied with a flourish. "Everything is in perfect working order."

* * *

For a holiday, Hamish decided to go to Switzerland to realise a lifelong ambition to climb the Matterhorn. He hired a guide, and just as they neared the top, the men were caught in a snow slide. Three hours later, a Saint Bernard ploughed through to them, a keg of brandy tied under his chin.

"Hooray!" shouted the guide. "Here comes man's best friend!"

"Yes," said Hamish. "And look at the size of the dog that's bringing it!"

* * *

Two City ladies were discussing their vacation plans on a London street corner within earshot of a Cornish lady.

"We're planning a lovely holiday in Cornwall this year," said one.

"Oh you shouldn't do that," said the other, "there are Cornish people there! It would be awful."

"Dear me!" said the first lady.

"Well, where are you going?"

"Landsend," she replied.

"But Landsend is simply crawling with Cornish people!" the first objected. At this point the Cornish lady could no longer hold her tongue. "Why don't ye go t' hell?" she suggested. "There are no Cornish people there!"

* * *

A man and his wife were driving through Anglesey and were nearing Llanfair P.G. (the longest town name in Wales). They noted the spelling and tried to figure how to pronounce it: Llan–fair–pwll–gwyn-gyll… They grew more perplexed as they drove into the town.

Since they were hungry, they pulled into the shop next to the station where they could get something to eat. At the counter, the man said to Megan, the waitress, "My wife and I can't seem to be able to figure out how to pronounce the name of this place. Will you tell me where we are and say it very slowly so that I can understand?"

Megan looked at him and said: "Prrrr-iingng-glllle-sssss." *

* * *

A tourist gets into a taxi outside Cardiff station. After a few minutes, when they were passing the castle, the tourist taps the taxi driver gently on the shoulder. With that, Dai the driver swerves over the kerb, nearly hits the bus shelter, mounts the verge, swerves back and rejoins the road. After a short silence, Dai turns to his passenger and says, "Don't you ever do that again".

"Sorry," said the passenger. "I didn't mean to upset you, but please tell me what I did wrong."

"Well," said Dai, "I suppose it's not really your fault, but I'm new to this job as a taxi driver. Before this job, I'd been driving a hearse for 15 years."

* * *

Dai got a job on an ocean liner as a conjuror and magician, and upon performing one night, the Captain's parrot kept on interrupting his act by betraying his trade secrets with comments such as "it's up his sleeve," "it's behind his ear," and so on.

Whatever trick Dai performed, the parrot kept his beady eye on it and gave the show away to the audience.

---

* Pringles – a famous shop in the centre of Llanfair P.G.

One evening, during the show, the ship hit an iceberg and started to sink. Dai managed to jump overboard and found a plank to cling onto. Soon afterwards, the parrot landed on the same plank.

For the next two days, they just stare at one another, until in the end the parrot chirps, "OK, I give up. What have you done with the bloody ship?"

* * *

Ianto is walking along Penarth beach and finds a bottle. He naturally rubs it, and lo and behold, a genie appears. "I will grant you three wishes," announces the genie. "But since Satan still hates me, for every wish you make, your rival Brynley gets the wish as well – only double."

Ianto thought about this for a while. "For my first wish, I would like £10 million quid," he announced. Instantly the genie gave him a Swiss bank account number and assured him that £10 million had been deposited.

"But Brynley has just received £20 million," the genie said.

"I've always wanted a Ferrari," Ianto said. Instantly a Ferrari appeared.

"But Brynley has just received two Ferraris," the genie said. "And what is your last wish?"

"Well," said Ianto, "I've always wanted to donate a kidney for transplant."

* * *

A plane leaving Cardiff airport passes through a severe storm. The turbulence is awful, and things go from bad to worse when one wing is struck by lightning. Betty, in particular, loses it. Screaming, she stands up in the front of the plane.

"I'm too young to die!" she wails. Then she yells, "Well, if I'm going to die, I want my last minutes on earth to be memorable! I've had plenty of sex in my life, but no one has ever made me really feel like a woman! Well, I've had it! Is there anyone on this plane who can make me feel like a woman?"

For a moment there is silence. Everyone has forgotten their own peril, and they all stare, riveted, at the desperate Betty in the front of the plane.

Then, Meirion stands up in the rear of the plane. "I can make you feel like a woman," he says. He's gorgeous. Tall, well-built, with curly black hair and jet black eyes, he starts to walk slowly up the aisle, unbuttoning his shirt one button at a time. No one moves. Betty is breathing heavily in anticipation as Meirion approaches. He removes his shirt. Muscles ripple across his chest as he reaches her, and extends the arm holding his shirt to the trembling Betty, and whispers in a sexy voice: "Iron this."

* * *

# Armed Forces

During the Second World War, a German spy was trained to go to the Rhondda.

"We need to keep an eye on what the British are up to," said the Herr Kommandant. "We will parachute you into the Rhondda, where you will go to the local town and ask for Dai Evans. He is your contact. You will say to him, 'The weather could change by Tuesday'."

The German duly landed in the Rhondda, buried his parachute and set off for Ponty. On the way he saw a local farm worker in a field.

"Güten morg... I mean, good morning. Vould you know vair I can find Mister Dai Evans?"

"Well, sir," answers the man. "It all depends on which Dai Evans you want. We have a Dai Evans Above – the preacher; a Doctor Dai Evans; Dai Evans the post-office; Dai Evans the plumber and, as a matter of fact – my name is also Dai Evans."

"Oh mein Gott!" thinks the German. Then he has an idea. He says, "The weather could change by Tuesday!" A beatific smile of recognition illuminates the Welshman's face. "Ah," says he, "You'll be wanting Evans the Spy!"

\* \* \*

A large group of English soldiers are moving up a road not far away from Bannockburn in 1314 when they hear a voice call from behind a hillock: "One Scottish soldier is better than ten English!"

The English general quickly sends ten of his best soldiers over the hill, whereupon a mighty battle breaks out and continues for a few minutes, and then there is silence.

The voice then calls out, "One Scottish soldier is better than twenty English!"

Furious, the English general sends his next best twenty troops over the hill and instantly a huge battle commences. After ten minutes of battle, again silence. The voice calls out again, "One Scottish soldier is better than one hundred English!"

The enraged English general musters one hundred fighters and sends them across the hill. The sound of a massive battle is heard. Then silence. Eventually one wounded English fighter crawls back over the hill, and with his dying words tells his general, "Don't send any more men. It's a trap. There are two of them."

# Marriage

Judge Evans has his shoes in his hand and is sneaking out of the house when his wife Marged catches him.

"And where do you think you're sneaking off to?" she demands.

"Oh, my dear, I almost forgot to tell you – there's a political meeting at the County Social Club this evening and I have to attend as it is about my judgeship."

"Evans bach, if you get drunk, I'll be leaving you."

"Oh, no cariad – this is strictly a political meeting."

And off Evans goes for a night out with the boys. He comes home arseholed at 2 a.m., balls his clothes up, throws them in the laundry, gets fresh clothes, catches a few winks on the couch and sneaks out before Marged wakes up.

At 9.30 a.m. during a court case, the clerk of the court slides a note onto the bench. The note reads, "It's your wife, she says it's urgent!" So Judge Evans calls a recess and goes into his office to call home.

"You bloody liar, Evans!" screams an enraged Marged. "Didn't I warn you that if you went out drinking, we'd split up?"

"But cariad! There was no drinking."

"Then what's this sick doing all down the front of your suit, shirt and necktie?"

"But cariad, I nearly forgot to tell you – when I came out of the meeting there was this terrible drunk that came up and vomited right over me. But I called the police and they threw him into a cell and he'll be up before me this morning. I'll give that boyo thirty days in jail for his trouble!"

"Well, see that you do!"

At 10.00 a.m. Judge Evans is still hearing cases when the clerk of the court slides another note onto the bench. The note reads, 'It's your wife again, she says it's urgent!' Judge Evans calls another recess and goes into his office to call home.

"Has that terrible drunk been up before you – the one that's going to get thirty days in jail?"

"No cariad, but when he comes up – it's thirty days for him!"

"No darling, give him ninety days," says Marged.

"That seems excessive – why ninety days?"

"Because he shit your pants, too!"

\* \* \*

Mick came home drunk very late every evening. Now, his poor wife was not too happy about it, either. So one night she hid in the cemetery so as to scare the living daylights out of him. As poor Mick wanders by, his wife jumps up from behind a gravestone in a red devil costume, screaming, "Mickey O'Reilly, sure and if ya don't give up your drinkin' and it's to hell I'll take ye".

Mick, undaunted, staggered back and demanded, "Who the hell are you?"

To that the figure replied, "I'm the devil, ya damned old fool". To which O'Reilly remarked, "Damned glad to meet you, sor, I'm the one who married your sister".

\* \* \*

Gerwyn and Beryl – both members of Treorchy Young Farmers' Club – got married, and they just couldn't seem to get enough loving. Just before leaving the house for the fields at dawn, they made love, and when Gerwyn returned home at evening they had another go – both before and after supper, and then again a few more times during the night.

The problems only arose during the day. The fields were far

away from the house and Gerwyn would lose half an hour each time travelling home and back again at noon. Finally he decided to consult the doctor about what to do.

"Easiest thing in the world, Gerwyn," said the doctor. "You take your shotgun out with you every day, don't you? Well, when you feel like you're in the mood for some loving, just fire a shot into the air as a signal to Beryl, for her to come out to you. That way you won't lose any working time."

Gerwyn tried the Doctor's solution and it seemed to work pretty well for a while. One day, though, the doctor stopped by the house to pay a visit and he noticed Gerwyn sitting alone inside looking very sombre.

"What's wrong?" he asked, "Didn't my idea work? And where's Beryl?"

"Oh, it worked," said Gerwyn. "Whenever I got in the mood I fired off a shot like you said, and Beryl would come running. Then we'd find a secluded place and make love. Then Beryl would go back home."

"So what's the problem?"

"Well I think I overdid it, Doc. I ain't seen hide nor hair of Beryl since the glorious twelfth."

\* \* \*

Ianto aged 92, and Rebecca, 91 are all excited about their decision to get married. They go for a walk to discuss the wedding and on the way they pass a chemist's shop. Ianto suggests they go in, and the following exchange ensues:

Ianto: We're about to get married. Do you sell heart medication?
Pharmacist: Of course we do.
Ianto: How about medicine for circulation?
Pharmacist: All kinds.
Ianto: Medicine for rheumatism?
Pharmacist: Definitely.
Ianto: How about Viagra?

Pharmacist: Of course.

Ianto: Medicine for memory problems, arthritis, jaundice?

Pharmacist: Yes, a large variety. The works.

Ianto: What about vitamins, sleeping pills, geritol?

Pharmacist: Absolutely.

Ianto: You sell wheelchairs and walkers?

Pharmacist: All speeds and sizes.

Rebecca speaks up and says to the pharmacist: "We'd like to register here for our wedding gifts, please."

\* \* \*

Huw Treharne was in court for non-payment of maintenance to his ex-wife. The judge decided to increase his wife's allowance. So he told Huw, "I have decided to increase this allowance and give your wife £50 a week". Huw replied, "You're a gentleman, sir, and I might even send her a few bob myself".

\* \* \*

During their silver anniversary, Megan reminded Ianto: "Do you remember when you proposed to me, I was so overwhelmed that I didn't talk for an hour?" Ianto replied: "Yes, cariad, that was the happiest hour of my life".

\* \* \*

When Ifor and Megan get married, Ifor asks if he can have his own drawer in the dresser, and that Megan will promise never to open it. Megan promises. After 25 years of marriage, she notices that the drawer has been left open. She takes a quick look inside and sees three golf balls and about £1,000 cash.

She confronts Ifor and asks for an explanation. He explains, "Every time I was unfaithful to you, I put a golf ball in the drawer". She calculated that three times in 25 years wasn't all that bad, as there had been some very happy times. However she asked, "But what about the £1,000 cash?"

"Whenever I got a dozen golf balls, I sold them for a pound," Ifan explained.

* * *

Gerwyn and Rhiannon arrive home from hospital after the birth of their first baby, and Rhiannon suggests to Gerwyn that he should try changing the baby's nappy.

"I'm busy at the moment," replied Gerwyn. "I'll change the next one."

Sometime later Rhiannon asks again.

"No," says Gerwyn, "I meant the next baby."

* * *

"Have you ever seen one of those new machines that can tell when a person is telling a lie, Hamish?"

"Seen one? I married one!"

* * *

Mary and Twm were in a restaurant and ordered fish. The waiter brought a dish with two fish, one larger than the other. Mary said, "Help yourself". Twm said "Okay," and helped himself to the larger fish. After a tense silence, Mary said, "Really, now, if you had offered me first choice, I would have taken the smaller fish!" Twm replied, "What are you complaining for; you've got what you wanted, haven't you?"

* * *

Evan, an elderly gent, was invited to his old butty Gwilym's home for dinner one evening. He was impressed by the way his buddy Evan preceded every request to his wife Myfanwy with a loving pet name. The couple had been married for almost 70 years, and clearly they were still very much in love. While Myfanwy was in the kitchen, Evan leaned over to Gwilym and said, "I think it's wonderful that after all these years, you still call Myfanwy those loving pet names." Evan hung his head. "Is that her name? To tell you the truth," he said, "I forgot her name about ten years ago."

# Tightfistedness

Angus called in to see his friend Donald to find he was stripping the wallpaper from the walls. Rather unnecessarily, he remarked, "You're decorating, I see." To which Donald replied, "Och no, man. I'm moving house."

\* \* \*

Old Tam – who had lost all his teeth – was visited by the minister, who noted that Tam had a bowl of almonds.

"My brother gave me those, but I don't want them. You can have them," said Old Tam. The minister tucked into them and then said, "That was a funny present to give a man with no teeth." Old Tam replied, "Not really; they had chocolate on them".

\* \* \*

Callum called his father-in-law 'the Exorcist' because every time he came to visit, he made the spirits disappear.

\* \* \*

A farmer's wife, who was rather stingy with her whisky, was giving her shepherd a drink. As she handed him his glass, she said it was extra good whisky, being fourteen years old. "Weel, mistress," said the shepherd regarding his glass sorrowfully, "It's very small for its age."

\* \* \*

At an auction in Glasgow, a wealthy American announced that he had lost his wallet, which contained £10,000, and would give a reward of £100 to the person who found it. From the back of the hall a Scottish voice shouted, "I'll give £150!"

* * *

Jock's nephew came to him with a problem. "I have my choice of two women," he said. "A beautiful, penniless young girl whom I love dearly, and a rich old widow whom I can't stand."

"Follow your heart; marry the girl you love," Jock counselled.

"Very well, Uncle Jock," said the nephew. "That's sound advice."

"By the way," asked Jock, "where does the widow live?"

* * *

"I hear Maggie and yourself settled your difficulties and decided to get married after all," Jock said to Sandy.

"That's right," said Sandy, "Maggie's put on so much weight that we couldn't get the engagement ring off her finger."

* * *

Have you heard about the lecherous Jock who lured a girl up to his attic to see his etchings? He sold her four of them.

* * *

A Scotsman took a girl for a ride in a taxi. She was so beautiful he could hardly keep his eye on the meter.

* * *

Twm Twice, a Cardigan Farmer, was looking for a Christmas gift for a friend. Everything was too expensive except for a vase that was broken, which he could buy for almost nothing. He asked the store to send it, hoping his friend would think it had been broken in transit. In due time, he received a reply. "Dear Twm, thanks for the vase," it read. "It was thoughtful of you to wrap each piece separately."

* * *

"I hear you're a great believer in free speech."

"I am at that, Iorwerth."

"Well, do you mind if I use your phone?"

* * *

"It was like this," said Iestyn. "I was teaching the wife to drive, and the brakes failed when we came down the hill."

"What did you tell her?"

"Try and hit something cheap!"

* * *

It was a terrible winter – three months of unbroken blizzards. McTavish hadn't been seen in the village for weeks, so a Red Cross rescue team struggled to his remote croft at the head of the glen. It was completely buried – only the chimney was visible.

"McTavish," they shouted down the chimney. "Are you there?"

"Wha's that?" came the answer.

"It's the Red Cross," they called.

"Go away," shouted McTavish. "I bought a flag last year!"

* * *

"You always get screwed when you buy a used van from a Cardi," said Arwyn Jones to his wife Meirwen.

"That settles it!" she yelled. "I'm going out to buy a used van from a Cardi."

* * *

The following advertisement appeared in a Scottish newspaper: "A gentleman who has lost a left leg would like to correspond with another who has lost his right leg and takes a size nine shoe."

* * *

Then there were two Cardis who bet a pound on who could stay underwater the longest. Both drowned.

* * *

A Cardigan undertaker sent a telegram to the bereaved Evan, telling him his mother-in-law had died, and asking whether he wanted her embalmed, cremated, or buried. Back came the reply: 'All three – don't take any chances.'

* * *

How do you disperse an angry Scottish mob?
Take up a collection.

* * *

A Cardigan farmer was out working the field when a barnstormer
landed. "I'll give you an airplane ride for £5," said the pilot.

"Sorry, I can't afford it," replied the farmer.

"Tell you what," said the pilot, "I'll give you and your wife a free
ride if you promise not to yell. Otherwise it'll be £10."

So up they went and the pilot rolled, looped, stalled and did all
he could to scare the Cardi. Nothing worked and the defeated
pilot finally landed the plane. Turning around to the rear seat he
said, "Gotta hand it to you. For country folk you sure are brave!"

"Aye," said the farmer, "But you nearly had me there when my
wife fell out!"

* * *

How was the Grand Canyon created?
A Scotsman lost a sixpence.

* * *

Mrs Angus McCafferty came into the newsroom to pay for her
husband's obituary. She was told by the kindly receptionist that it
was 10p a word. She thanked her for her kind words, and
bemoaned the fact that she only had 20p. But she wrote out the
obituary: 'Angus died'. The receptionist said she thought old
Angus deserved more, and that she'd give her three more words at
no extra charge. Mrs McCaffery thanked her and rewrote the
obituary: 'Angus died. Bagpipes for sale'.

* * *

Ianto had worked all of his life and had saved hard, and he was a
real miser when it came to his money. He loved money more than
just about anything, and just before he died, he said to his wife,
"Now listen. When I die, I want you I want you to take all my

money and put it in the coffin with me. I want to take my money to the grave with me."

And so he got Myfanwy to promise him with all her heart that when he died, she would put all the money in the coffin with him. Well, sure enough, he died. He lay stretched out in the casket; Myfanwy was sitting there in black, and her friend Megan was sitting next to her. When they finished the ceremony, just before the undertakers got ready to close the casket, Myfanwy said, "Wait just a minute!' She had a box with her, and she brought it over and put it in the coffin. Then the undertakers screwed the coffin down, and they rolled it away.

Megan said, "Myfanwy fach, I know you weren't fool enough to put all that money in there with your late husband."

"Listen, I'm a good woman," Myfanwy said. "I can't go back on my word. I promised my Ianto that I was going put that money in that coffin with him."

"You mean to tell me you put that money in the coffin with him?"

"Certainly," said Myfanwy. "I wrote him a cheque."

(Note: a month later, the cheque was cashed; the undertaker was from Ceredigion as well!)

* * *

A young Ceredigion boy and girl were sitting on a low stone wall, holding hands, gazing out over Ceredigion Bay. For several minutes they sat silently. Then finally the young girl looked at the boy and said, "A penny for your thoughts, Gareth."

"Well, uh, I was thinking. Perhaps it's about time for a little kiss." The girl blushed, then leaned over and kissed him lightly on the cheek. Then Gareth blushed. The two turned once again to gaze out over the bay.

Minutes passed and the girl spoke again. "Another penny for your thoughts, Gareth".

"Well, uh, I was thinking perhaps it's now about time for a small cwtsh." The girl blushed, then leaned over and cuddled him for a few seconds. Then Gareth blushed. Then the two turned once again to gaze out over the Irish sea.

After a while, she again said, "Another penny for your thoughts, Gareth."

"Well, uh, I was thinking perhaps it's about time you let me put my hand on your leg." The girl blushed, then took his hand and put it on her knee. Then Gareth blushed, and the two turned once again to gaze out over the sea before the girl spoke again.

"Another penny for your thoughts, Gareth."

Gareth glanced down with a furled brow. "Well, now," he said, "my thoughts are a little bit more serious this time."

"Really?" said the young girl in a whisper, filled with anticipation.

"Yes," said Gareth, nodding. The young girl looked away in shyness, began to blush, and bit her lip in anticipation of the ultimate request. Then Gareth said, "Do you not think it's about time you paid me the first three pence?"

\* \* \*

Rabby finds himself in dire trouble. His business has gone bust and he's in serious financial problems. He's so desperate that he decides to ask God for help. "God, please help me. Ah've lost ma wee store and if ah dinna get some money, ah'm going to lose my hoose too. Please let me win the lottery!"

Lottery night! Someone else wins. Rabby prays again. "God, please let me win the lottery! Ah've lost my wee store, ma hoose and ah'm going to lose ma car as weel!"

Lottery night again! Still no luck. Rabby prays again. "Ah've lost ma business, ma hoose and ma car. Ma bairns are starving. Ah dinna often ask Ye for help and ah have always been a good servant to Ye. Please just let me win the lottery this one time so ah can get back on ma feet!"

Suddenly there is a blinding flash as the heavens open and the voice of God Himself thunders: "Rabby, at least meet me half way and buy a ticket!"

\* \* \*

A Scottish newspaper classified ad: "Lost – a £5 note. Sentimental value".

# A Welshman, a Scotsman, an Irishman... and an Englishman

An Irishman, a Welshman and an Englishman are caught drinking in Saudi Arabia.

"Under Saudi law you are sentenced to thirty lashes followed by deportation. Before the punishment begins, you are entitled to have something on your back. What would you like?" said the prison guard to the Englishman just before lashing him. The Englishman, being a bit of a cricket addict, asked for linseed oil. They lashed him to a post, and after the punishment, he groaned and crawled to one side. Next came the Welshman. "Under Saudi law you are sentenced to thirty lashes followed by deportation. Before the punishment begins, you are entitled to have something on your back. What would you like?" said the prison guard to the Welshman.

"Nothing," he replied. "In the Rhondda we are all tough." After receiving his lashes he spat on the ground and called the prison guards diawled. The guards then came to the Irishman. "Under Saudi law you are sentenced to thirty lashes followed by deportation. Before the punishment begins, you are entitled to have something on your back. What would you like?" said the prison guard to the Irishman.

"Oh," he replied, "I'll take the Englishman".

\* \* \*

There were three men – a Welshman, a Scotsman, and an Irishman – and all three were on a hike through the woods, and they knew they had to stop to set up camp for the night. Taffy suggested they stop where they were right there; a nice clear, wooded area. Jock agreed, but Paddy disagreed, because there was nothing interesting around, only trees.

They kept hiking for a little longer, and came across a small clear area, right next to the highway. Both Jock and Taffy wanted to stay there because there was no stumps or moss around, and the sounds of the cars could help put them asleep. Patrick said no, because he found a small anthill some 500 yards away, and was scared the ants might come and get them. So they kept hiking, and finally they came to the end of the woods and stepped onto the highway. Patrick was elated, and wanted to sleep right smack in the middle of the road, as he wanted to look at all the different registration numbers, as they drove by. Taffy and Jock were not so keen, because obviously that was the last place that they wanted to settle down in, but they were too tired to argue, so they agreed with Paddy to set up their tent in the middle of the road, and went to sleep.

They slept soundly through the night, but were woken a couple of times by the sound of cars beeping, and crashing. The next morning, when they woke up, they noticed a huge pile-up of cars right off the road, in the spot they had earlier chosen.

Feeling proud, Paddy said: "See, boys? I told you that this was the safest place. You can see what would have happened if we'd slept over there last night!"

* * *

A Scotsman, a Welshman and an Englishman are walking along the seashore when they find an antique oil lamp. They rub it and a genie comes out in a puff of smoke. The genie says, "I usually only grant three wishes, so I'll give you one each."

"Me first! Me first!" says the Scotsman. "I want to be in the Bahamas, driving a speedboat, without a care in the world." Poof! He's gone.

"Me next! Me next!" says the Welshman in astonishment. "I want to be in Hawaii, relaxing on the beach with my personal masseuse, an endless supply of Brains beer and the love of my life." Poof! He's gone.

"OK, you're up," the genie says to the Englishman.

"Oh… It's kind of lonely here now that they've gone… I wish they were back here."

* * *

A Scottish man, an Englishman and an Irishman were sitting in a pub discussing the best pubs around. The Englishman says, "There's a pub in the West Midlands where the landlord buys you a pint for every one that you buy." The Scot is not impressed and says, "That's nothing! In the Highlands every time you buy a drink the landlord buys you five drinks." The Englishman is very impressed with that. The Irishman, however, is totally unimpressed and says, "That's nothing. In Dublin there's this pub where the landlord buys you drinks all night, and then when the bar shuts, he takes you into a room where you can make love all night long." The Scot and Englishman are well impressed and ask the Irishman if he goes there a lot. He replies, "No, my sister told me about it."

* * *

An Englishman, a Scotsman and an Irishman were without tickets for the opening ceremonies of the summer Olympics but hoped to be able to talk their way in at the gate. Security was very tight, however, and each of their attempts was met with a stern refusal. While wandering around outside the stadium, the Englishman came upon a construction site, which gave him an idea. Grabbing a length of scaffolding, he presented himself at the gate and said, "Johnson, the pole vault," and was admitted. The Scotsman, overhearing this, went at once to search the site. When he came up with a sledgehammer, he presented himself at the gate and said,

"McTavish, the hammer." He was also admitted. The Irishman combed the site for an hour and was nearly ready to give up when he spotted his ticket in. Seizing a roll of barbed wire, he presented himself at the gate and announced, "O'Sullivan, fencing."

\* \* \*

An English politician was giving a speech in Aberystwyth. "I was born an Englishman, I have been an Englishman all my life, and I will die an Englishman!" he declared.

"What's wrong, boyo?" exclaimed a voice from the crowd. "Got no ambition, 'ave you?"

\* \* \*

An air freight flight flying across the Atlantic to America was carrying four passengers: A Welshman, a Scotsman, an Englishman, and an Irishman. They'd almost reached their destination near Australia, when one of the plane's four engines caught fire.

"Don't worry!" said the pilot, as he activated the fire extinguishers and feathered the prop. "This plane was designed to fly on just two engines. We'll be fine!"

A little while later, an engine on the other wing coughed and sputtered and stopped. The plane appeared to be slowly losing altitude when the pilot came on the intercom and said: "Don't worry, men; this plane can still fly on two engines, but we're going to have to lighten the load."

The co-pilot came back into the cabin and opened a rear door. He then directed the five men in helping to jettison the crates that the plane was carrying. Once all the crates were out, he secured the door and went back to the forward cabin. The plane still appeared to be losing altitude. The pilot came back on the intercom and said, "I'm sorry gentlemen, but the plane's still too heavy and I'm going to have to ask some of you to jump out. There are parachutes in a storage cabinet. We are still over the sea, but I will radio ahead and try to have someone send a rescue boat out to get you." The co-pilot came back to the main cabin, dug out the parachutes from a storage cabinet, stacked them up next to the side door and opened it.

The Irishman jumped up, grabbed a parachute, strapped it on, walked to the door, turned to the others, shouted "God Bless Ireland!" and jumped out. The co-pilot called the pilot on the intercom, but the pilot said the plane was still too heavy. He turned around and looked at the remaining three men. "I'm sorry guys, but someone else is going to have to jump!"

The Scotsman sighed and stood up next, strapped on a parachute, strode to the door, yelled "Scotland the Brave!" and without looking back, jumped out. The co-pilot checked with the pilot again only to hear him say they were still too heavy. The co-pilot looked from the Englishman to the Welshman and said, "Gentlemen, someone else has to go. You have a decision to make. I think one more just might do it!" The Welshman jumped up and said, "Not a problem!" He grabbed the Englishman by the collar, dragged him to the door, shouted, "Cymru am Byth!" and threw him out the door without a parachute.

* * *

One day an Englishman, a Scotsman, and an Irishman walked into an Edinburgh pub together. They each bought a large glass of the low flyer. Just as they were about to enjoy the wee dram, a fly landed in each of their glasses, and was swimming in the whisky. The Englishman pushed his drink away in disgust. The Irishman fished the fly out of his whisky, and continued drinking it, as if nothing had happened. The Scotsman, too, picked the fly out of his drink, held it out over the glass, and started yelling, "SPIT IT OUT, SPIT IT OUT YOU BASTARD!"

* * *

A Scotsman and an Englishman were having a magnificent meal at one of the finest restaurants in London. At the end of the evening the waiter came over to present the bill, and a Scottish voice said, "That's all right, laddie, just gae the bill to me". The headlines in the local newspaper next day proclaimed 'English ventriloquist found beaten to death'.

\* \* \*

Mick is sitting in a tavern one night when three Englishmen walked in, sat down, and started to mutter about how they could wind the Irish fellow up. The first man says, "Watch this." He gets up, walks over to Mick, and says, "Hey man, I hear your St Patrick was a faggot." Mick just replied, "Oh, is that so?"

The Englishman goes back to his seat perplexed, and his friend jumps up and says, "Here, let me try that." So he goes over to Mick and says, "Hey man, I hear your St Patrick was a transvestite faggot!" The Irishman replies mildly, "Oh, is that so?"

The frustrated Englishman returns to sit down with his friends. The third Englishman jumps up and says, "Well, now, I can do better than that!" So he walks over to Mick and says, "Hey, I hear your St Patrick was an Englishman!" And Mick replies, "Aye, that's what your mates said".

\* \* \*

A Scotsman and a Englishman were flying from Edinburgh when the stewardess approached them. "May I get you something?" she asked.

"Aye, a whisky," the Scotsman replied. She poured him a drink then asked the Englishman if he'd like one.

"Never!" he said sternly. "I'd rather be raped and ravished than drink whisky!"

The Scotsman hurriedly passed the drink back, saying "Och, Ah didna ken there wuz a choice!"

\* \* \*

Five Englishmen boarded a train just behind five Scots, who as a group had only purchased one ticket between them. Just before the conductor came through, all the Scots piled into the toilet stall at the back of the car. As the conductor passed the stall, he knocked and called, "Tickets, please!" and one of the Scots slid a ticket under the door. It was punched, pushed back under the door, and when it was safe all the Scots came out and took their seats. The Englishmen were tremendously impressed by the Scots' ingenuity. On the trip back, the five Englishmen decided to try this themselves and purchased only one ticket. They noticed that, oddly, the Scots had not purchased any tickets this time. Anyway, again, just before the conductor came through, the Scots piled into one of the toilet stalls, the Englishmen into the other. Then one of the Scots leaned out, knocked on the Englishmen's stall and called "Tickets, please!" When the ticket slid out under the door, he picked it up and quickly closed the door.

* * *

Once upon a time, the BBC decided to send a Welshman, a Scotsman and an Irishman to a desert island for two years. The BBC allowed each of them to take 200 lbs of baggage each. The Welshman decided to take along his wife; the Scotsman decided to take along books to learn how to speak proper English; the Irishman decided to take along 200 lbs of cigarettes. Two years later, when they returned, there was a big crowd waiting to welcome them home. First came the Welshman and his wife and each of them had a baby in their arms. Next came the Scotsman speaking fluent English with an Oxford accent. They both gave their speeches and got a rousing round of applause. Suddenly, out came the Irishman with a cigarette in his mouth. He walked up to the podium, snarled at the crowd, and asked "Has anyone got a bloody match?"

* * *

A building contractor hires a Scotsman, an Irishman, and a Chinaman. He gathers them all in his office and tells each of them their jobs. The Scotsman has to shovel a pile of sand. The Irishman has to take the sand in the wheelbarrow to the truck. The Chinaman is in charge of supplies.

The boss comes back two hours later and he sees the Scotsman and the Irishman having a cup of tea. "So have you done the work, then?" he asks. The workers both shake their heads and tell him that the Chinaman didn't give them a shovel or a wheelbarrow. The boss is infuriated by this and asks the workers if they have seen the Chinaman. They reply that they thought they saw him going toward the truck. So the boss sets out towards the truck and just as he is getting close to the truck the Chinaman jumps out from behind a wall and yells, "Supplies!"

* * *

When Hamish moved to London he constantly annoyed his English colleagues by boasting about how great Scotland was. Finally, in exasperation, one said, "Well, if Scotland's so bloody marvellous, how come you didn't stay there?"

"Well," replied Hamish, "they're all so clever up there I had to come down here to have any chance of making it at all."

* * *

An Englishman and an Irishman are driving head on at night on a dark, twisty road. Both are driving far too fast for the conditions and collide with each other on a sharp bend in the road. To each one's surprise, both are unmarked, though both cars are a write-off. To celebrate their amazing good fortune, they agree to put aside their differences from that moment on. At this point, Paddy goes to the boot and fetches a bottle of twelve-year-old Jameson's whiskey. He hands the bottle to the Englishman, who exclaims, "May the English and the Irish live together forever in peace and harmony". The Englishman then tips the bottle and lashes half of it down. Still flabbergasted over the whole thing, he hands the bottle to Paddy, who says, "No thanks, I'll just wait for the garda to get here first!"

\* \* \*

Recently, Scotland conducted some scientific exploration involving their best scientists. Core drilling samples of earth were taken to a depth of 50m, and small pieces of copper were discovered. After running many arduous tests on these samples, the Scottish government announced that the ancient Scots of 25,000 years ago had a nationwide telephone network.

Naturally, the British government was not that easily impressed. So they ordered their own scientists to take core samples at a depth of 100m. From these samples, they found small pieces of glass and soon announced that the ancient Brits of 35,000 years ago already had a nationwide optical fibre network.

Irish scientists were outraged. So immediately after this announcement, they ordered their scientists to take samples at a depth of 200m but found absolutely nothing. They concluded that the ancient Irish of 55,000 years ago were an even more advanced civilisation, as they already had a mobile telephone network in place.

\* \* \*

Three men are sitting in the maternity ward of a hospital waiting for the imminent birth of their respective children. One is an Englishman, one a Welshman and the other a Jamaican. They are all very nervous and pacing the floor. All of a sudden the doctor bursts through the double doors saying,

"Gentlemen, you won't believe this, but your wives have all had their babies within five minutes of each other." The men are beside themselves with happiness and joy. "And," said the doctor, "they've all had little boys."

The fathers are ecstatic and congratulate each other over and over.

"However, we do have one slight problem," the doctor said. "In all the confusion, we may have mixed the babies up getting them to the nursery, and we'd be grateful if you could join us there to try and help identify them."

With that the Welshman raced past the doctor and bolted to the nursery. Once inside he picked up a dark-skinned infant with dreadlocks, and said, "There's no doubt about it, this boy is mine!" The doctor looked bewildered and said, "Well, sir, of all the babies, I would have thought that this child is the one most obviously of Jamaican descent."

"True," said the Welshman, "but there's a 50 50 chance that one of the others is English, and I'm not taking the risk."

\* \* \*

On a tour of Wales, the Pope took a couple of days off his itinerary to visit the west coast near the Gower on an impromptu sightseeing trip. His 4x4 Popemobile was driving along the golden sands when there was an enormous commotion heard just off the headland. They rushed to see what it was and upon approaching the scene, the Pope noticed just outside the surf a hapless man wearing an English rugby jersey, struggling frantically to free himself from the jaws of a twenty-foot shark.

At that moment a speedboat containing three men wearing Welsh rugby tops roared into view from around the point. Spontaneously, one of the men took aim and fired a harpoon into the shark's ribs, immobilising it instantly. The other two reached out and pulled the Englishman from the water and then, using long clubs, beat the shark to death.

They bundled the bleeding, semi-conscious man into the speedboat along with the dead shark and then prepared for a hasty retreat, when they heard frantic shouting from the shore. It was, of course, the Pope, and he summoned them to the beach. Upon their reaching the shore, the Pope went into raptures about the rescue and said, "I give you my blessing for your brave actions. I had heard that there were some racist people trying to divide Wales and England, but, now I have seen with my own eyes this is not true. I can see that your society is a truly enlightened example of racial harmony and could serve as a model which other nations could follow." He blessed them all and drove off in a cloud of dust.

As he departed, the harpoonist asked the others, "Who was that?"

"That," one answered, "was his Holiness the Pope. He is in direct contact with God and has access to all God's wisdom."

"Well," the harpoonist retorted, "he knows fuck all about shark hunting. How's that bait holding up – do we need to get another one?"

\* \* \*

An Englishman is walking down the main street of Ballykissangel and meets Liam standing on the pavement beside a big strong horse. This prompts the Englishman to attempt to realise a lifelong dream and he says to Liam, "Say, that's a fine-looking horse you've got there, and I'd like to tour this beautiful country on horseback so that I can see the sights and hear the sounds of the countryside, like they did in the old days. I'll buy that horse off you – how much do you want for him?"

"Oh sure, and you don't want to be messin' with this horse. He don't look too good these days."

"Hey, boy!" says the Englishman. "Don't you try to tell me what's a good-looking horse and what isn't. I've been trading horses all my life and there's nothing a young country boy like you can tell me about them. Now you just name your price and we'll get along fine."

"I'm sayin' to ye that this horse is not a good-lookin' horse, mister and ye don't want any part of 'im," says Liam. The

Englishman is getting angry now.

"Listen, boy!" he says. "You let me be the judge of what's good-looking and what's not, and just give me the price and I'll pay cash right here and now."

"Oh well," says Liam. "2,000 punts."

"Deal!" says the Englishman and he hands over the money. Liam unties the horse and the Englishman leads him off. The horse walks smack into the first lamp post in the way, and the Englishman turns to Liam and says, "Hey, boy! You're a damned swindler! You didn't tell me this horse was blind!"

"I keep tellin' you he don't look too good," says Liam, "and you kept saying that's none of my business, so in the end I gave up."